Eight Principles For Happyness

The Beatitudes of Jesus for Today

H. Carl Shank

Eight Principles for Happyness: The Beatitudes of Jesus for Today

ISBN 978-0-359-57282-3

Cover design: H. Carl Shank. "Morning, Sky, Sunlight, Flower" by ID 114296424 © Publicdomainphotos | Dreamstime.com. "Happyness" is not a misspelling but intentional.

First Edition 2019

Printed in the United States of America

About the Author

In addition to his M.Div. and Th.M. (systematics) work, H. Carl Shank has been a youth, associate, solo, staff and lead pastor in over forty years of church ministry, pastoring beginning and established congregations in Pennsylvania, Delaware, Maryland, Virginia and New York state. His passion for leadership development has resulted in mentoring numerous pastors, teaching in a number of local Bible institutes as well as serving as an adjunct faculty member of The King's College, and training InterVarsity leaders on the East Coast. Carl has been regularly sought out for his acknowledged gifts of discernment and wisdom in dealing with church issues. He had been serving as the Executive Pastor of a church in Lancaster, PA, as well as a church health consultant through NCDAmerica. He is recently retired.

Besides numerous seminars and church related articles, his recently published Bible study contributions include *Living Life God's Way: Reflections from the Psalms, Study Guide and Leader's Guide, Romans: The Glory of God As Seen in the Righteousness of God, Jonah: A Reluctant Messenger, A Needy People, and God's Amazing Grace, Esther: For Such A Time As This, A Study of God's Providence, Church Warnings! The Seven Churches of Revelation for Today, Building For God: Leadership and Life Lessons from Nehemiah, The Pastoral Letters Revisited: Behavior and Belief,* and *Authentic Christianity: The Message to the Thessalonians,* all available from Lulu Press, Amazon and other booksellers. Carl is married to his wonderful wife, Nancy, and has three grown, married children. He lives in the Marietta, PA area and can be reached for consulting, seminars or leadership and mentoring development at

cshanktype@gmail.com
www.carlshankconsulting.com

Table of Contents

Other Titles by the Author

Foreword

Probably the most famous, if not the most quoted, sermon from the lips of Jesus is the Sermon on the Mount. This sermon has been quoted for and against conservative Bible students. Its ethics have been favorably used by many different religions in a variety of settings and ways.

I was first introduced to the Sermon on the Mount by the writings of possibly the most famous preacher in the United Kingdom in the twentieth century, Dr. Martyn Lloyd Jones.[1] His notes and insights to this sermon by Jesus need read and re-read by everyone for their incisiveness and correct biblical theology. Their practical application cannot be easily escaped or put aside for the serious student of Scripture or the modern church goer. Additionally, I have found the older Puritan writers a treasure trove of practical application on the Sermon.

This study guide covers what are called the beatitudes of Jesus in Matthew 5:3–12. These eight (or nine, if verses 11 and 12 are not seen as an additional explanation of the eighth) are simple, direct and fundamental ethical foundations to all of life. They each begin with the opening word "happy" or "blessed," and then give the reason for such a distinction. Luke's Gospel (Luke 6:20–22) highlights only four of the beatitudes "balanced by four 'woes'. They are phrased in the second person and focus on the material and social condition of the disciples, rather than on the spiritual qualities set out here."[2]

Matthew Henry quaintly says, "Blessed Jesus! how different are thy maxims from those of men of this world! They call the proud happy, and admire the gay, the rich, the powerful, and the victorious. May we find mercy from the Lord; may we be owned as his children, and inherit his kingdom. With these enjoyments and hopes, we may cheerfully welcome low or painful circumstances."[3] John Calvin notes, "Let us, therefore remember, that the leading object of the discourse is to show, that those are not unhappy who are oppressed by the reproaches of the wicked, and subject to various calamities. And not only does Christ prove that they are in the wrong, who measure the happiness of man by the present state, because the distresses of the godly will soon be changed for the better; but he also exhorts his own people to patience, by holding out the hope of a reward."[4] Often, these beatitudes have been looked upon by those enamored with the Puritans from a negative point of view. According to them, we live mostly unhappy lives, toiling against the adversities of the world, the flesh and the Devil. The beatitudes are written, therefore, for our comfort in a harsh and darkened world of sin and shame.

A deeper and richer look into these beatitudes grants us a view of genuine and lasting happiness, the "good life," as one writer puts it.[5] Jesus understands fully the negatives in life, but his concern in these eight or nine ethical lessons is to cheer us and tell us what real, lasting and genuine happiness is all about. That is the approach of this study of the beatitudes.

Carl Shank

2019

Notes

1.   Martyn Lloyd Jones, *Studies in the Sermon on the Mount* (London: InterVarsity Press and Wm. B. Eerdmans, 1959-60, 1971, 1976, reprinted 2000), 9–148.

2.   Gordon J. Wenham (Editor), J. Alec Motyer (Editor), Donald A. Carson (Editor), R. T. France (Editor), *New Bible Commentary* (IVP Academic, 1994), 906ff, https://www.accordancebible.com/.

3.   Matthew Henry, *Matthew Henry's Concise Commentary on the Whole Bible* (Thomas Nelson, 2003), https://www.accordancebible.com/. Notably "gay" in Matthew Henry's day did not have a homosexual orientation, but rather meant lighthearted, carefree to the point of foolishness.

4.   John Calvin, *Calvin's Commentaries*, https://www.studylight.org/commentaries/cal/matthew-5.htm.

5.   *New Bible Commentary* on Matthew 5:3ff.

Happyness
The Good Life According To Jesus

"Seeing the crowds, he went up on the mountain, and when he sat down, his disciples came to him. And he opened his mouth and taught them, saying: "Blessed are . . ."
(Matthew 5:1ff ESV)

Happyness. No, it is not a misspelling or a reference to a recent movie outlining the life of a homeless man and his son who worked from destitution to riches.[1] I am using this spelling to distinguish what Jesus is talking about here in the beatitudes from the general notion of happiness.

A Google search of "how to be . . ." will reveal "happy" as one of the first choices for which people are looking. For most, happiness is a feeling of contentment and emotional satisfaction over their circumstances. People want to feel good about themselves and their situations. Happiness depends on happenings. They want to be secure in the old notion that "I'm okay, and you're okay." But is this what Jesus is talking about in the opening to the Sermon on the Mount in Matthew 5?

Religionists would point out that the word Jesus uses as recorded in the Bible is "blessed." That puts a seemingly sacred context to his ethical sayings. However, Jesus uses a more popular word *makarios*. The Greek word was as old as that of Homer and the Iliad which calls the gods of Olympus "happy" in the sense that they were not, like mortal men, subject to the restrictions and vicissitudes of fate or chance.[2] Happiness was related to outward prosperity and good circumstances.

Jesus lifts the idea of happyness beyond and above such common notions of the day and identifies it with kingdom oriented spiritual character —

"Shaking itself loose from all thoughts of outward good, it becomes the express symbol of a happiness identified with pure character. Behind it lies the clear cognition of sin as the fountainhead of all misery, and of holiness as the final and effectual cure for every woe. For knowledge as the basis of virtue, and therefore of happiness, it substitutes faith and love" (Vincent). Jesus takes this word "happy" and puts it in this rich environment. "This is one of the words which have been transformed and ennobled by New Testament use; by association, as in the Beatitudes, with unusual conditions, accounted by the world miserable, or with rare and difficult" (Bruce).[3]

To the Jewish audience of the day, Jesus reminds them of the Old Testament word which referenced a "happy" person who "walks not in the counsel of the wicked, nor stands in the way of sinners, nor sits in the seat of scoffers." (Psalm 1:1) Happy are those who take refuge in the promised Son of God (Psalm 2:12), whose sin is forgiven by God (Psalm 32) and who hope in the Lord (Psalm 34:8; 40:4; 84:12). That nation is "happy" whose God is the LORD Jehovah (Psalm 33:12) — "Happy are you, O Israel! Who is like you, a people saved by the LORD, the shield of your help, and the sword of your triumph! Your enemies shall come fawning to you, and you shall tread upon their backs." (Deut. 33:12)

Consequently, true happyness took on an ethical cast —

But in harmony with the Deuteronomistic view, happiness depends on the choice (Ps. 33:12) or teaching of God (94:12). The believer must fear God (112:1; 128:1). His behavior must be blameless (119:1f.), and he must obey the Torah and not follow the counsel of the wicked (1:1). Happy is he who considers the poor (41:2[1]), who observes justice and does "righteousness" (106:3), who receives sons as a gift from God in his youth (127:5), and who executes God's judgment against the enemies of the chosen people (137:8).[4]

In other words, it is the life of a person living out the covenantal relationship between God and his people. Happyness is deeper and more expansive than what we expect or suspect. The disciples are "happy" because they see and hear what many religious people of their day refused to see and hear — "But blessed are your eyes, for they see, and your ears, for they hear." (Matt. 13:16) "And Jesus answered him, "Blessed are you, Simon Bar-Jonah! For flesh and blood has not revealed this to you, but my Father who is in heaven." (Matt. 16:17)

It is a pity that we have not kept the word "happy" to the high and holy plane where Jesus placed it. "If you know these things, happy (*makarioi*) are you if you do them" (John 13:17). "Happy (*makarioi*) are those who have not seen and yet have believed" (John 20:29). And Paul applies this adjective to God, "according to the gospel of the glory of the happy (*makariou*) God" (1 Tim. 1:11. Cf. also Titus 2:13). The term "Beatitudes" (Latin *beatus*) comes close to the meaning of Christ here by *makarioi*. It will repay one to make a careful study of all the "beatitudes" in the New Testament where this word is employed.[5]

The kingdom of heaven and happyness

Notice that Jesus brackets such happyness with character qualities of the kingdom of heaven — "Blessed are the poor in spirit, for theirs is the kingdom of heaven. . . . Blessed are those who are persecuted for righteousness' sake, for theirs is the kingdom of heaven." (Matt. 5:3, 10)

The Dutch theologian Herman Ridderbos has caught the importance of the gospel of the kingdom which Jesus preached —

At first sight the gospel of the kingdom of heaven consists of two parts which together form an unbreakable unity. The first part is related to the *gift*, the *salvation*, given in the gospel; the other part is related to the *demand*, the *command* in which it is expressed . . the gift of salvation preached thus also contains a command, and that, conversely, the command, the demand of the kingdom also belongs to the salvation proclaimed by Jesus. . . . Just as in that great and glorious example of Jesus' preaching of the kingdom, viz., the Sermon on the Mount, we find first the beatitudes and afterwards the commandments.[6]

The beatitudes were not entirely new, consequently, to the people on the mount. They were the fulfillment of what is old. Salvation and life in the kingdom of God is "terminologically and factually determined by the history of the revelation preceding it, and cannot be understood apart from it."[7]

When Jesus came to this earth and said, "The time is fulfilled, and the kingdom of God is at hand; repent and believe in the gospel," (Mark 1:15), he was delivering happyness to people who would see, hear and believe. He as Lord was proclaiming that his sovereign rule and lordship now encompassed the whole of created reality. Those people are happy who believe in King Jesus and follow the word of this King.

Happy people in King Jesus are happy when they are at the end of their rope, when they feel they've lost what is most dear to them only to be embraced by the One most dear to them, when they are content with just who they are, when they have a good appetite for God, when they care, when they get their inside world put right, when they show people how to cooperate instead of compete and fight, when their commitment to God provokes persecution, and when people put them down or throw them out or speak lies about them to discredit them. (Matthew 5:3–11 *The Message*) It doesn't matter, consequently, what the present, and most likely, miserable, state of people were or are today. They can be really and truly and deeply happy in this new kingdom of Jesus.

> From this definition we may learn, that the person whom Christ terms happy is one who is not under the influence of fate or chance, but is governed by an all-wise providence, having every step directed to the attainment of immortal glory, being transformed by the power into the likeness of the ever-blessed God. Though some of the persons, whose states are mentioned in these verses, cannot be said to be as yet blessed or happy, in being made partakers of the Divine nature; yet they are termed happy by our Lord, because they are on the straight way to this blessedness.[8]

If this does not describe the followers of Jesus you may know, then they may have missed the overwhelming joys of the kingdom of God and being with Jesus. One of my most respected mentors in the faith in college was a local pastor who had been at his Reformed Baptist church for many years. He schooled me in the doctrines of grace and Reformed theology and gave me a love for the Puritans. Yet, near the end of his ministry I recall sitting in his office with him telling me that his one regret in ministry and in his pastorate was that he wished there was more joy among the people.

This statement at the time amazed me because this man was a carefully trained biblical scholar and expositional preacher. He had preached through the Bible a number of times. But he had bought into the mindset that true Christians and true Christianity was serious, sober and not to be taken lightly. He and his congregation, unfortunately, had missed the happyness that Jesus taught here in the beatitudes.

J. R. Miller writes about gaining the habit of cheerfulness —

There are few habits more common, even among Christians, than this of remembering the unpleasant things and forgetting the pleasant things; and there is no other habit which is more inimical to joy. He who would always be of good cheer must break this habit — if it has fastened itself in his life — and must learn, must train himself, to see the beautiful things and to be blind to the disagreeable things. The truth is, there are, in the ordinary life, a thousand pleasant things — favors, joys, comforts, things to cheer — to one unpleasant thing, one real cause for unhappiness. It is a shame, therefore, to let the one bit of roughness, trial or suffering spoil all the gladness of the thousand blessings, the one discordant note mar all the music of the grand symphony. We should learn to look at life, not to find misery and discomfort in it, but to find cheer and beauty.[9]

You and I live in the era of the kingdom of Jesus. Theologians call this a partially realized kingdom (tasiology)[10] to be finally and fully revealed when Jesus returns. We still have the residual effects of sin and shame and misery with which to deal, but we deal with them in the hopeful realization that King Jesus is with us and will most certainly return.

We can therefore be happy in the salvation gift that Jesus gives to all who simply believe and follow him and confident that as we follow the commands and word of this King we will find contentment, satisfaction and hope.

Spin cheerfully, not tearfully,
Though wearily you plod;
Spin carefully, Spin prayerfully,
But leave the thread with God.

The shuttles of His purpose move
To carry out His own design.
Seek not too soon to disapprove
His work, nor yet assign
Dark motives, when, with silent dread,
You view each somber fold;
For, lo! within each darker thread
There twines a thread of gold.

Spin cheerfully, not tearfully,
He knows the way you plod;
Spin carefully, Spin prayerfully,
But leave the thread with God.
(Anonymous)

Self Reflection & Discussion

1. Are you "happy?" How would you define or describe this happiness?
2. Are you a child of King Jesus? How does this knowledge affect your emotional states?
3. Are you comfortable with Jesus beginning his ministry with the word "happy?" Why or why not?
4. Do you believe Christianity and Christians should be more "serious" rather than more happy? Why or why not?

Notes

1. Steven Conrad, "The Pursuit of Happyness," filmed December 15, 2006 by Columbia Pictures, an American biographical drama film based on entrepreneur Chris Gardner's nearly one-year struggle being homeless. Directed by Gabriele Muccino, the film features Will Smith as Gardner, a homeless salesman. Smith's son Jaden Smith co-

stars, making his film debut as Gardner's son, Christopher Jr., https://en.wikipedia.org/wiki/The_Pursuit_of_Happyness.

2.   "Homer, Iliad i, 330, calls the supreme gods, Θεων μακαρων, the ever happy and Immortal gods, and opposes them to θνητων ανθρωπων, mortal men," from *Adam Clarke's Commentary* on Matthew 5, https://www.studylight.org/commentaries/acc/matthew-5.html.

3.   Quoted in A.T. Robertson, *Word Pictures in the New Testament* (Broadman Press, 1930), on the word *makarios*.

4.   Henri Cazelles, *Theological Dictionary of the Old Testament* (TDOT), ed. G. Johannes Botterweck and Helmer Ringgren, trans. John T. Willis, Vol. 1 (Grand Rapids: Eerdmans, 1974), 445-448, article on "blessing" [אשרי].

5.   Robertson, *Word Pictures*.

6.   Herman Ridderbos, *The Coming of the Kingdom*, trans. H. de Jongste, Raymond Zorn, ed. (New Jersey: Presbyterian and Reformed Publishing Company, 1969), 186.

7.   *Ibid*.

8.   *Adam Clarke Commentary* on Matthew 5.

9.   J. R. Miller, Quotations On "Cheerfulness" from *Pearls From Many Seas*, Compiled by Rev. J. B. McClure, SAGE Software Albany, OR USA Version 1.0, 1995.

10.   Tasiology or semi-eschatology is the "already/not yet" pattern of eschatology [doctrine of last things] inaugurated by Jesus at his first coming — "The two-episode kingdom-coming-event corresponds to Jesus' first and second comings: once in humiliation and once in glory. With the ascension of the risen Christ into heaven, the preeminent arena of the Spirit, the administration of His priestly-kingdom and its redemptive blessings are removed from our sight (hid with Christ in God). Thus, Christ's heavenly session presently is the firstfruits presence of the age to come. Moreover His death on the cross was an intrusion of the final judgment and His resurrection from the dead an intrusion of the new creation, both eschatological events. Believers, entering into union with Him in those events, have been translated from the kingdom of this world into the kingdom of our Lord. Thus, because He has overcome and lives never to die again, believers in Him partake of all the blessings of His resurrection life, "blessed with every Spiritual blessing in the heavenly places in Christ," and "seated with Him in the heavenlies."

The situation created by the postponement of the consummation-event is an overlap of the ages. In Christ the age to come, the new creation, the kingdom, has become a present reality. This overlap of the ages is illustrated by Geerhardus Vos's two-age diagram (See Below). The two-age construction helps us to understand what God yet promises to do for man through the revelation of what God has already done by Jesus Christ, to Jesus Christ, and through Jesus Christ. In other words, the two-age worldview recognizes God's own personal coming in Jesus Christ as the particular and definitive, final (i.e. eschatological) action of God for saving His people from their sins and bringing many sons to glory. Man cannot truly apprehend himself eternally before the loving presence of Jehovah Adonai unless he is first apprehended by God through Christ's own once-for-all death-resurrection-ascension. In this manner, we understand that Christ's advent and finished work to have inaugurated the kingdom of God, the eschatological arena-age for all those given entrance by the Holy Spirit

through faith, even while this present evil world-age continues for a time." (http://
two-age.biblicaltheology.org/beliefs_index/eschatology.htm)

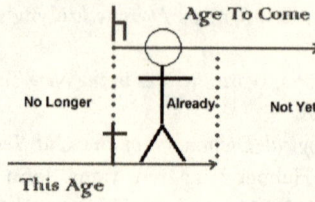

Poverty Of Spirit
Happy Are The Oppressed

"Blessed are the poor in spirit, for theirs is the kingdom of heaven."
"You're blessed when you're at the end of your rope. With less of you
there is more of God and his rule."
(Matthew 5:3 ESV, NIV, KJV and The Message)

Jesus began his earthly ministry with the Old Testament call to the poor — "The Spirit of the Lord is upon me, because he has anointed me to proclaim good news to the poor. He has sent me to proclaim liberty to the captives and recovering of sight to the blind, to set at liberty those who are oppressed, to proclaim the year of the Lord's favor." (Luke 4:18, 19 from Isaiah 61:1, 2) "Go and tell John what you have seen and heard: the blind receive their sight, the lame walk, lepers are cleansed, and the deaf hear, the dead are raised up, the poor have good news preached to them." (Luke 7:22) Good news to the poor, the oppressed, the downtrodden of society. This was certainly a welcome message to most of the people in Jesus' day, and such news has been used in our day to give hope and life to millions of the world's poor and despised.

But in spite of the translators who champion such a thought, is this what Jesus meant? Did he indeed pronounce happiness on all the world's poverty stricken peoples? Did he go on to say that for the poor and oppressed of our world, theirs would be the kingdom of heaven and final deliverance and joy? Is this universal happiness promised by Jesus?

The terms Jesus uses, "poor" (*ptoochos*) and "poor in spirit" (*ptoochos tooi pneumati*)[1] agree with the Hebrew *ani* and *anaw*.[2] Both words talk about external distress or oppression and the humility of the sufferer in distress (cf. Luke 4:18; 6:20; 7:22; Psalm 18:28; 72:2; 74:19). The Old Testament background to the poor under distress or oppression gives important parameters to what Jesus is teaching here in this first beatitude.

God's concern for the poor helps us to remember of his great mercy for his own! The "poor" in the Old Testament illustrated the importance of what it meant to be "poor in spirit". We need the LORD for all things. We are utterly dependent upon his goodness for the sun and the rain, as well as for all material blessings (Matthew 6:24-33). In fact, Jesus will later teach in the Sermon on the Mount that God knows of our great needs, and will meet them and so there is absolutely nothing to fear or worry about![3]

Jesus in the fulfillment of his role as the incarnation of the coming of God's kingdom came for those who had been designated "poor in spirit" in the Psalms and the Prophets.

They represent the socially oppressed, those who suffer from the power of injustice and are harrassed by those who only consider their own advantage and influence. They are, however, at the same time those who remain faithful to God and expect their salvation from his kingdom alone. They do not answer evil with evil, nor oppose injustice with injustice. That is why in the midst of the ungodliness and worldlimindedness of others, they form the true people of God. As such they are again and again comforted with the promise of the coming salvation of the Lord and the manifestatio of his kingly redemption (cf. Ps. 22:27; 25:9; 34:3; 37:11; 72:12, 13; 147:6; Isaiah 11:4; 29:19, etc).[4]

In this redemptive-historical sense, they expect the salvation God has held out to his people as the "consolation of Israel" (Luke 2:35; cf. 6:24; 16:25; Matt. 5:4). This is not a universal salvation for all oppressed for all time, however. "On the contrary, this message is purposely adapted to the special relationship which God has established between himself and his people. . . . It is the reality of God's covenant and of his theocratic relationship to Israel as his people which is the basis of the description of the gospel as the gospel of the poor. It is this true people of God which is addressed in the beatitudes and to whom the salvation of the kingdom is granted as their lawful right."[5]

The above understanding offered by the Dutch theologian Herman Ridderbos in his thesis, *The Coming of the Kingdom*, has specifically textual and biblical historical appeal.[6] But it does not take away from the ethical need for those who would be considered recipients of the kingdom of God to have the character trait of poverty of spirit. Anyone who evidences the traits of poverty of spirit is welcome into the kingdom of Jesus Christ.

Helpful understanding of poverty of spirit comes from reading the Puritans on this topic, especially Thomas Watson.[7] Watson made several important distinctions while talking about this verse. He noted that not all poverty is blessed and went on to make four distinctions.

Poverty of spirit is not merely *situational* or *locational* poverty, what he calls "poverty of estate" — "There are the Devil's poor. They are both poor and wicked—whose clothes are not more torn than their conscience. There are some whose poverty is their sin, who through improvidence or excess have brought themselves to poverty."[8] Just because a person lives in a poor environment or in a poor part of the world does not make him or her poor in spirit. Jesus is not speaking to all the environmentally poor of our age. This is crucial since a number of modern mainline denominations have made the help and elimination of poverty and the oppressed an important part of their gospel message, what evangelicals have called the "social gospel."

In college InterVarsity Christian Fellowship, we had a girl from a mainline denominational background who volunteered for digging ditches in South America under the auspices of the Peace Corps. She challenged the group to have "real" gospel outreach to the oppressed of the world, rather than just proclaiming the gospel of grace in the Word of God to others. She felt very strongly that the gospel must be hands-on to be truly Good News. Other evangelical means of witness were insufficient and ineffective, she believed.

While I admired her zeal and commitment to the poor and oppressed of this world, her replacement of the Good News with good deeds does not accord with the fullness of the gospel preached and taught by Jesus. The "poor in spirit" are not merely the disadvantaged and oppressed of this world.

Watson also notes poverty of spirit is not referencing those who may be merely "spiritually poor" — "He who is without grace is spiritually poor—but he is not poor in spirit; he does not know his own beggary. 'You know not, that you are poor' (Revelation 3:17)."[9] There are a lot of "spiritually poor" people who do not know or recognize their need of a Savior from sin. In fact, they see themselves as "okay" and not needing this Jesus of the Bible. They have no sense of need of Christ. These are not "poor in spirit."

Poverty of spirit is not being "poor-spirited," mean and selfish hoarders "who live sneakingly, and are ready to wish their own throats cut, because they are forced to spend something in satisfying nature's demands. This Solomon calls an evil under the sun (Ecclesiastes 6:2)."[10] He goes on to further delineate "those who act below themselves as they are Christians, while they sinfully comply and prostitute themselves to the desires of others; a base kind of metal that will take any stamp. They will for a piece of silver—part with the jewel of a good conscience. They will be of the popular religion. They will dance to the devil's pipe, if their superior commands them. These are poor-spirited but not poor in spirit."[11]

Finally, Jesus is not speaking to those who bask in voluntary poverty — "those who, renouncing their estates, vow a voluntary poverty, living retiredly in their monasteries. But Christ never meant these. He does not pronounce them blessed—who make themselves poor, leaving their estates and callings—but such as are evangelically poor."[12]

Rather, Watson says, Jesus refers to "those who are brought to the sense of their sins, and seeing no goodness in themselves, despair in themselves and sue wholly to the mercy of God in Christ. Poverty of spirit is a kind of self-annihilation. 'The poor in spirit' (says Calvin) 'are those who see nothing in themselves—but fly to mercy for sanctuary.'"[13]

The Message translation of this verse has it right — "With less of you there is more of God and his rule." Such was the spirit of the ancient tax collector in Luke 18:13 — "But the tax collector, standing far off, would not even lift up his eyes to heaven, but beat his breast, saying, 'God, be merciful to me, a sinner!'" Such was the testimony of the converted Apostle Paul — "and be found in him, not having a righteousness of my own that comes from the law, but that which comes through faith in Christ, the righteousness from God that depends on faith." (Phil. 3:9) Such are the poor who are invited as guests to the wedding banquet of the King of kings —"Blessed are those servants whom the master finds awake when he comes. Truly, I say to you, he will dress himself for service and have them recline at table, and he will come and serve them. If he comes in the second watch, or in the third, and finds them awake, blessed are those servants!" (Luke 12:37, 38)

What are those traits, those characteristics that make a person "poor in spirit?" He knows, first of all, that he *needs the grace of Christ*. He is aware of his need of the Savior of the world. He or she knows that to depend on themselves is not merely unsatisfactory, but to no avail, not only for eternity but also for the here and now. This is not a "poor me" or "woe is me" attitude as it is a resolute and heartfelt dependence on Christ alone for spiritual, emotional and mental health and vitality.

People who evidence this poverty of spirit *value Christ above all else*. "'The pearl of great price' is only precious to the one who is poor in spirit. He who needs bread and is ready to starve, will have it whatever it cost. He will lay his garment to pledge; bread he must have—or he is undone! So to him who is poor in spirit, who sees his need of Christ—how precious is a Savior! Christ is Christ and grace is grace to him! He will do anything for the bread of life!"[14]

And such is Christ's blood—it can never be emptied. He who is poor in spirit has recourse still to this fountain. He sets a high value and appreciation upon Christ. He hides himself in Christ's wounds. He bathes himself in his blood. He wraps himself in Christ's robe. He sees a spiritual dearth and famine at home—but he flees to Christ. 'Show me the Lord (says he) and it suffices!'"[15] While this may seem quite "old school" to many professing Christians of our day, it accurately represents those who live in poverty of spirit.

A third note would be that those who practice poverty of spirit understand the *upside down nature of kingdom of God living* — "How poor are those who think themselves rich! How rich are those who see themselves poor! I call it the 'jewel of poverty'. There are some paradoxes

21

in piety which the world cannot understand; for a man to become a fool that he may be wise (1 Corinthians 3:18); to save his life by losing it (Matthew 16:25); and by being poor to be rich."[16]

Perhaps poverty of spirit is best said in an old hymn —

> Rock of Ages, cleft for me,
> Let me hide myself in Thee;
> Let the water and the blood,
> From Thy riven side which flowed,
> Be of sin the double cure,
> Save me from its guilt and power.
>
> Not the labor of my hands
> Can fulfill Thy law's demands;
> Could my zeal no respite know,
> Could my tears forever flow,
> All could never sin erase,
> Thou must save, and save by grace [alone].
>
> Nothing in my hands I bring,
> Simply to Thy cross I cling;
> Naked, come to Thee for dress,
> Helpless, look to Thee for grace:
> Foul, I to the fountain fly,
> Wash me, Savior, or I die.
>
> While I draw this fleeting breath,
> When mine eyes shall close in death,
> When I soar to worlds unknown,
> See Thee on Thy judgment throne,
> Rock of Ages, cleft for me,
> Let me hide myself in Thee.
> (Augustus Montague Toplady, 1740-1778)

Self Reflection & Discussion

1. How can a person be "poor in spirit" and yet be happy? Isn't it an oxymoron to talk of the "happy poor?"

2. Do a concordance study of "poor" in the Old Testament. Was Jesus speaking to such in his Sermon on the Mount?

3. Of the three major characteristics of poverty of spirit, with which one do you have the most difficulty in your Christian life? Why?

4. Sing or listen to the hymn, "Rock of Ages, Cleft For Me." Let the words speak to you.

Notes

1. The Greek terms are πτωχοὶ, πτωχοὶ τῷ πνεύματι.

2. The Hebrew term is עֲנִי.

3. Charles R. Biggs, "The Beatitudes: Matthew 5:1–12," *Reformed Perspectives Magazine*, Volume 5, no. 43, December 1 to December 7, 2003.

4. Herman Ridderbos, *The Coming of the Kingdom*, trans. H. de Jongste, Raymond Zorn, ed. (New Jersey: Presbyterian and Reformed Publishing Company, 1969), 188-189.

5. Ridderbos, 192. Such thinking could possibly be adopted by Dispensationalists who understand the Beatitudes of Jesus to be ethical teachings for the nation of Israel during the coming millennial reign of Christ (cf. Rev. 20). They make a harsh distinction between the Church and the nation of Israel.

6. Ridderbos takes issue with the major theological writers of his day in his understanding of the "poor in spirit." It is not primarily an "ethical-religious conception of the kingdom of heaven," (Harnack) nor the "absolutely objective, transcend character of the kingdom" where the "poor" are "the sinners" (Bultmann) that is at work here. "Generally speaking, it may be said that in the recent literature on the subject the view prevails that the contents of the gospel do not have an immanent-ethical meaning, but are intended in a transcendent-soteriological sense.," of which Ridderbos disagrees (187ff).

7. Thomas Watson, *The Beatitudes: An Exposition of Matthew 5:1-12*, 1660, Monergism eBook, https://www.monergism.com/topics/free-ebooks.

8 – 16. Watson, "Poverty of Spirit," *The Beatitudes*.

Joyful Mourning
The Second Beatitude

"Blessed are those who mourn, for they shall be comforted."
"You're blessed when you feel you've lost what is most dear to you. Only
then can you be embraced by the One most dear to you."
(Matthew 5:4 ESV, NIV, KJV, The Message)

We need to remind ourselves that these eight or nine beatitudes are not eight or nine "pick and choose" categories of the Christian life. They are not separate, distinct blessings to be chosen by the way we feel, or the way we operate, or dependent on our personalities or preferences.

They are the normal part of living for Jesus. They are for the average person who says he or she loves and knows Jesus Christ as Savior and Lord. In other words, they are not "super qualities" for the "more sanctified," or the "more religious," or the more "in tune" with God. They are not merely for the Christian elite of the world or the church. These are the qualities for all who have claimed allegiance to Jesus and profess to be Christ-followers. They are the fundamental markers of kingdom of God living in our day. God counts such people as "happy" travelers in the journey to heaven and glory. They live with fundamental satisfaction with God and in the world around them. As John Piper has well said, "God is most glorified in us when we are most satisfied in him."

Joyful mourning. Isn't that an oxymoron, like the "living dead," or "bitter sweet," or "accidently on purpose," or "pretty ugly?" Shakespeare strings them together in *Romeo and Juliet* — "O heavy lightness! Serious vanity! Misshapen chaos of well-seeming forms!"[1] How can a mourner be happy? If what you have lost in your life is most dear to you, how can you be fundamentally satisfied with your life? Clearly, these are the questions that this second beatitude raises.

"Those who mourn." This is a reminder of and a direct allusion to Isaiah 61 — "The Spirit of the Lord GOD is upon me, because the LORD has anointed me to bring good news to the poor; he has sent me to bind up the brokenhearted, to proclaim liberty to the captives, and the opening of the prison to those who are bound; to proclaim the year of the LORD's favor, and the day of vengeance of our God; to *comfort all who mourn.*" (Isa. 61:1, 2) Jesus as the King ushers in the Messianic age where the downtrodden seeking justice and comfort find it in him.

Here the key word (πενθοῦντας) is exactly the same as in the beatitude. Thus again we find the eschatological expectation of the downtrodden and poor, those who suffer. The rabbis accordingly referred to the Messiah as the "Comforter" (Měnahēm) because of his mission in the messianic age (cf StrB 1:195). Those who mourn do so because of the seeming slowness of God's justice. But they are now to rejoice, even in their troubled circumstances, because their salvation has found its beginning.[2]

Again, however, we must not lose the ethical and practical implications of what Jesus is saying in the second beatitude. In a broader context, "those who mourn" describes the state of a much older Private Ryan in the movie[3] —a deep, gnawing, gut-level sense of anguish and sorrow. It is a personal brokenness before God that grips the emotions and mind and heart. It may be grief over personal or corporate tragedy or disaster. For the follower of Jesus, it is deep grief over both sin we commit (inside sins) and those sins committed around us that deeply affect us (outside sins).

Contrition would be the old word or term here. The eleven disciples immediately after Jesus' crucifixion and death and right before they realized his resurrection evidenced such grief — "She went and told those who had been with him, as they *mourned* and wept." (Mark 16:10) After his initial betrayal, Peter "went out and wept bitterly." (Luke 22:62) In 1 Corinthians 5:2, Paul is admonishing the church at Corinth for putting up with gross sexual immorality in their midst of a man with his father's wife — "And you are proud?!! Shouldn't you rather have been *filled with grief* and have put out of your fellowship the man who did this?" James 4:9 tells us to "grieve, mourn and wail" over the sin of covetousness which causes quarrels and envy and strife. King David in the Old Testament daily wept over the death of his wayward son Absalom (cf. 2 Samuel 18:33).

Dr. John (Jack) Miller wrote in *Evangelism and Your Church* —

Too many of our church members may have been born again, but their knowledge of their sin and the grace of God is so shallow that, in a real way, they need the message of salvation to come into their hearts with something like first-time conversion. And there is also a sense in which even more mature believers must confess that the world and the love of material comforts are too much with them. The first commandment continuously reveals that I have an unlimited need for a reconciling Savior.[4]

Contrition is a brokenness over personal and corporate sins — "And I said: "Woe is me! For I am lost; for I am a man of unclean lips, and I dwell in the midst of a people of unclean lips; for my eyes have seen the King, the LORD of hosts!" (Isaiah 6:5) "Now when they heard this they were *cut to the heart,* and said to Peter and the rest of the apostles, "Brothers, what shall we do?" (Acts 2:37)

Mourning, however, is not hopeless grief or sorrow. It is sorrow without gloominess or moodiness. It is seriousness without sullenness. It is a relational, dynamic quality of living before God that is sensitive to God's holy character, sensitive to one's standing or state before this God, and sensitive to the heart of Jesus who wept both over the graveside of Lazarus and the judgment about to fall on Jerusalem. Such mourning is caused, as one preacher put it, by the eyelash of God brushing against the sensitive folds of the heart.

Dr. Martyn Lloyd Jones raises the question, Why is such mourning lacking in our day? He notes from his perspective several factors.[5] First, there is a false Puritanism that has replaced what the original Puritans taught, believed and practiced. False Puritanism displays a life that is always sad, sorrowful and under God's anger and conviction but never relieved of such a burden. This was not the Puritanism of Thomas Watson and the other seventeenth century Puritans.

Watson points to a fivefold mourning that is false and spurious.[6]

There is a mourning of despair, such as that felt and displayed by Judas, the betrayer of Jesus (cf. Matthew 27:3ff). There is a hypocritical kind of mourning, such as that of Saul before Samuel in 1 Samuel 15:24ff. There is a forced mourning, such as Cain's mourning — "Cain said to the LORD, "My punishment is greater than I can bear." (Genesis 4:13) There is an external mourning, not from the heart, but seen in the faces of people, such as the hypocritical religious teachers of Jesus' day — "And when you fast, do not look gloomy like the hypocrites, for they disfigure their faces that their fasting may be seen by others. Truly, I say to you, they have received their reward." (Matthew 6:16)

Finally, Watson notes a fruitless mourning, like the rich man in hell wanting to be comforted — "and in Hades, being in torment, he lifted up his eyes and saw Abraham far off and Lazarus at his side. And he called out, 'Father Abraham, have mercy on me, and send Lazarus to dip the end of his finger in water and cool my tongue, for I am in anguish in this flame.' But Abraham said, 'Child, remember that you in your lifetime received your good things, and Lazarus in like manner bad things; but now he is comforted here, and you are in anguish." (Luke 16:23–25)

Watson goes on to describe right gospel mourning. It is mourning that is spontaneous and free, spiritually correct in grieving over sins more than suffering for those sins —

> Our mourning for sin must be so great as to exceed all other grief. Eli's mourning for the ark was such that it swallowed up the loss of his two children. Spiritual grief must preponderate over all other grief. We should mourn more for sin than for the loss of friends or estate. We should endeavor to have our sorrow rise up to the same height and proportion as our sin does. Manasseh was a great sinner—and a great mourner. 'He humbled himself greatly' (2 Chronicles 33:12). Manasseh made the streets run with blood—and he made the prison in Babylon run with tears. Peter wept bitterly. A true mourner labors that his repentance may be as eminent as his sin.[7]

Lloyd Jones also notes the wrong use of superficial happiness to attract the unbeliever to Christ, a defective sense of sin among us and a defective doctrine of sin in the Church, as well as a failure to understand the true nature of Christian joy, what I have called "happyness" in chapter one. The lack of real, deep conviction of sin coupled with a shallow sense of joy has negated biblical mourning among us.

"Will be comforted."[8] What a powerful and wonderful promise of Jesus here to the forlorn, the desperate, the anguished and helpless. To the Jewish faithful who were the oppressed of Jesus' day it meant coming justice and salvation. To those in our day who own and feel their brokenness before God, Jesus promises comfort! But it is not just God making us feel good. No, this comfort is much deeper and wider and greater. The term Jesus uses here has a multiplicity of meanings and nuances in the New Testament. And this is very purposeful because different kinds of grief for different kinds of reasons need different kinds of solutions. The amazing thing is that God covers them all! I suggest four such kinds of comfort.

"Will be comforted" can mean "will be encouraged" — "When they had preached the gospel to that city and had made many disciples, they returned to Lystra and to Iconium and to Antioch, strengthening the souls of the disciples, *encouraging* them to continue in the faith, and saying that through many tribulations we must enter the kingdom of God. And when they had appointed elders for them in every church, with prayer and fasting they committed them to the Lord in whom they had believed." (Acts 14:21–23)

"Will be comforted" can mean "will be cared for" — "Blessed be the God and Father of our Lord Jesus Christ, the Father of mercies and God of all comfort, who *comforts us in all our affliction,* so that we may be able to comfort those who are in any affliction, with the comfort with which we ourselves are comforted by God. For as we share abundantly in Christ's sufferings, so through Christ we share abundantly in comfort too." (2 Corinthians 1:3–5)

"Will be comforted" can also mean "will be exhorted or rebuked" — "For you know how, like a father with his children, we exhorted each one of you and *encouraged* you and charged you to walk in a manner worthy of God, who calls you into his own kingdom and glory." (1 Thessalonians 2:11, 12)

"Will be comforted" could also mean "will be instructed" — "For an overseer, as God's steward, must be above reproach. He must not be arrogant or quick-tempered or a drunkard or violent or greedy for gain, but hospitable, a lover of good, self-controlled, upright, holy, and disciplined. He must hold firm to the trustworthy word as taught, so that he may be able to *give instruction* in sound doctrine and also to rebuke those who contradict it." (Titus 1:7–9)

This beatitude is powerfully rephrased by *The Message* — "You're blessed when you feel you've lost what is most dear to you. Only then can you be embraced by the One most dear to you." You're blessed that when truly broken, God gives you what you need the most.

Isaac Watts in a beautiful old hymn said it best —

> When I survey the wond'rous Cross
> On which the Prince of Glory dy'd,
> My richest Gain I count but Loss,
> And pour Contempt on all my Pride.
>
> Forbid it, Lord, that I should boast,
> Save in the Death of Christ my God:
> All the vain things that charm me most,
> I sacrifice them to his Blood.
>
> See from his Head, his Hands, his Feet,
> Sorrow and Love flow mingled down!
> Did ever such Love and Sorrow meet?
> Or Thorns compose so rich a Crown?
>
> His dying Crimson, like a Robe,
> Spreads o'er his Body on the Tree;
> Then am I dead to all the Globe,
> And all the Globe is dead to me.

Were the whole Realm of Nature mine,
That were a Present far too small;
Love so amazing, so divine,
Demands my Soul, my Life, my All.
(Isaac Watts, 1707)

Self Reflection & Discussion

1. Have I experienced brokenness before God? If not, why not?
2. Have I enjoyed the amazing encouragement of soul that only Jesus Christ can give?
3. Why not today — why not right now?

Notes

1.   William Shakespeare, *Romeo and Juliet*, Act 1, Scene 1, Line 170, in Oxford School Shakespeare, *Romeo and Juliet*, ed. Roma Gill (Oxford University Press, 1994 and 2001 reprint).

2.   Donald A. Hagner, *Matthew 1–13, Word Biblical Commentary*, Vol 33A, Bruce M. Metzger (Editor), David Allen Hubbard (Editor), Glenn W. Barker (Editor), John D. W. Watts (Series Editor), James W. Watts (Series Editor), Ralph P. Martin (Series Editor), Lynn Allan Losie (Series Editor) (Zondervan, 2015), 92ff.

3.   "*Saving Private Ryan* is a 1998 American epic war film directed by Steven Spielberg and written by Robert Rodat. Set during the Invasion of Normandy in World War II, the film is notable for its graphic portrayal of war, and for the intensity of its opening 27 minutes, which includes a depiction of the Omaha Beach assault during the Normandy landings. It follows United States Army Rangers Captain John H. Miller (Tom Hanks) and a squad (Tom Sizemore, Edward Burns, Barry Pepper, Giovanni Ribisi, Vin Diesel, Adam Goldberg, and Jeremy Davies) as they search for a paratrooper, Private First Class James Francis Ryan (Matt Damon), who is the last surviving brother of four servicemen." (https://en.wikipedia.org/wiki/Saving_Private_Ryan)

4.   C. John Miller, *Evangelism and Your Church* (Presbyterian and Reformed Publishing, 1985).

5.   Martyn Lloyd Jones, *Studies in the Sermon on the Mount* (London: InterVarsity Press and Wm. B. Eerdmans, 1959-60, 1971, 1976, reprinted 2000), on Matthew 5:4.

6.   Thomas Watson, "Gospel Mourning," *The Beatitudes: An Exposition of Matthew 5:1-12*, 1660, Monergism eBook, https://www.monergism.com/topics/free-ebooks.

7.   *Ibid.*

8.   "The verb παρακληθήσονται is a so-called divine passive, which assumes God as the acting subject (so too in the fourth, fifth, and seventh beatitudes)." (Hagner, *Word Biblical Commentary*, 93)

Practical Humility
The Third Beatitude

"Blessed are the meek, for they shall inherit the earth."
"You're blessed when you're content with just who you are—no more, no less. That's the moment you find yourselves proud owners of everything that can't be bought."
(Matthew 5:5 ESV, KJV, NIV, The Message)

How do you measure greatness? What is it in a person that causes you to remark, "That's a great man or woman?" We are talking about the third beatitude of Jesus, found in Matthew 5:5 — "Blessed are the meek, for they will inherit the earth." We want to investigate this term "meekness" since it is so misunderstood and undervalued in our day, as it was in Jesus' day. We want to understand what it means to "inherit the earth" and what that involves and includes, since obviously we're not talking about corporate or personal ownership of the land mass called earth.

But let's begin with great people. Possibly one of our most honored and most revered national heroes is, of course, Abraham Lincoln. We think of his humble beginnings, his tall, lanky stature, his agonizing oversight of the Civil War in the 1860s. We remember his speeches which are plastered on the walls of the Lincoln Memorial in Washington, D.C.

But his most shining moment of greatness came on a battlefield in Gettysburg at the Soldiers National Cemetery on the afternoon of Thursday, November 19, 1863. After a wonderful and stirring oration of over two hours by one of the most sought after speakers of his day, Edward Everett, Lincoln in 272 words, and three minutes, asserted our nation was "conceived in Liberty, and dedicated to the proposition that all men are created equal," that the "government of the people, by the people, for the people, shall not perish from the earth." Accounts of that day record that he was in ill health when he gave the speech that is regarded as the greatest speech ever made in the history of the United States.

So, greatness is not based on how intelligent one is, how gifted a person is in public speaking, how admired a person is or how long he or she is on the podium of the nation. Everyone remembers Abraham Lincoln and few recall Edward Everett.

Sir Edmund Hillary, was a New Zealand mountaineer, explorer and philanthropist. On May 29, 1953, Hillary became the first man to successfully climb the highest mountain in the world, Mount Everest. He and his Sherpa guide reached Everest's 29,028 foot summit, the highest point on earth, at 11:30 AM. As Hillary put it, "A few more whacks of the ice axe in the firm snow, and we stood on top ." Following his ascent of Everest, he devoted most of his life to helping the Sherpa people of Nepal through the Himalayan Trust, which he founded. Through his efforts, many schools and hospitals were built in Nepal.

There is a story told about Hillary in one of the Nepalese villages in which a much less prominent mountain climber saw Hillary with an ice pick in his hand. Wishing to impress the gathered villagers with his knowledge and skill at mountaineering, he took the ice pick from Hillary's hand and gave it back to him with these words, "This is the right way to handle an ice pick!" Hillary just graciously thanked him for the advice.

Sir Edmund Hillary was a great climber, a great humanitarian, a great man not because of his accomplishments or his claim to fame on Mount Everest, but his remarkable humility and his care for the neglected people of Nepal.

Then, of course, in all the lists of the greatest people in the world is Jesus Christ. He was and is a truly great person, not for his exploits, his miracles, his fame, but for his teaching, his humility, his love for people and his great self-sacrifice for the sins of the world. His definition of greatness, his statement about himself, is given in Matthew 11 — "Come to me, all who labor and are heavy laden, and I will give you rest. Take my yoke upon you, and learn from me, for I am *gentle* and lowly in heart, and you will find rest for your souls." (Matthew 11:28, 29)

The word "gentle" that Jesus uses is "meekness" — "Blessed are the gentle, for they will inherit the earth." But it seems like a contradiction, doesn't it? While we, and the world in which Jesus lived, valued strength and love of honor, Jesus tells us and shows us what values the kingdom of God stands by. Notice these "seeming" contradictions — "Say to the daughter of Zion, 'Behold, your *king* is coming to you, *humble*, and mounted on a donkey, on a colt, the foal of a beast of burden.'" (Matthew 21:5) "But as for you, O man of God, flee these things. Pursue righteousness, godliness, faith, love, steadfastness, *gentleness*. *Fight* the good fight of the faith. Take hold of the eternal life to which you were called and about which you made the good confession in the presence of many witnesses." (1 Timothy 6:11, 12)

The first quote the gospel writer, Matthew, pulls from the Old Testament prophecy of Zechariah 9:9 — "Rejoice greatly, O daughter of Zion! Shout aloud, O daughter of Jerusalem! Behold, your king is coming to you; righteous and having salvation is he, humble and mounted on a donkey, on a colt, the foal of a donkey." As Christ followers we are to *argue gently*, to defend the faith gently — "Be prepared to give an answer to everyone who asks you to give the reason for the hope you have. But do this with gentleness and respect." (1 Peter 3:15) Paul talks about conquering spiritual strongholds and demolishing arguments against Christianity in the "meekness and gentleness of Christ" in 2 Corinthians 10. The young leader, Timothy, is exhorted to talk with those who oppose his message about Jesus with gentleness in 2 Timothy 2:24, 25 — "And the Lord's servant must not be quarrelsome but kind to everyone, able to teach, patiently enduring evil, correcting his opponents with gentleness. God may perhaps grant them repentance leading to a knowledge of the truth."

Biblical wisdom and understanding is gentle wisdom — "Who is wise and understanding among you? By his good conduct let him show his works in the meekness of wisdom." (James 3:13) Christians are to "live gently" — "Put on then, as God's chosen ones, holy and beloved, compassionate hearts, kindness, humility, meekness, and patience." (Colossians 3:12)

What is biblical meekness or gentleness? It is not weakness or wimpishness. Or spinelessness. The Christ who created the atoms in the bodies of the Roman soldiers who nailed him to the cross and who could have obliterated the prideful Pharisees with a brush of his eyelash or a thought, instead chose to forgive and suffer. All for us.

"Meekness" is not mere human niceness or a biological knack of being easy-going. We make a big mistake if we think that is what Jesus means here in the beatitudes. Some peoples' personalities are just nice; they are the kind who would do anything for another person; they are naturally humanitarians and caring people. No, this kingdom quality or value of meekness or gentleness is something God gives and does inside of us when He transforms us and remakes us into what we call Christians. It is a fruit of the Holy Spirit in us — "But the fruit of the Spirit is love, joy, peace, patience, kindness, goodness, faithfulness, *gentleness*, self-control; against such things there is no law." (Galatians 5:22, 23)

A working definition of "meekness" would be "a true view of oneself expressing itself in attitude about myself and conduct toward others," a true view coming from God opening our eyes to see what we are really like, our ears to hear the message of Good News and redemption, and our hearts to understand the gospel and be saved and delivered from ourselves.

These "meek" will "inherit the earth." Well, what does that mean? Obviously, it is not the accumulation of things Jesus is talking about here. Jesus reaches back into the Psalms, back into Psalm 37, and takes his cues from there —

> "For the evildoers shall be cut off,
> but those who wait for the LORD shall inherit the land.
> In just a little while, the wicked will be no more;
> though you look carefully at his place, he will not be there.
> But the meek shall inherit the land
> and delight themselves in abundant peace.
> Better is the little that the righteous has
> than the abundance of many wicked.
> for those blessed by the LORD shall inherit the land,
> but those cursed by him shall be cut off.

Turn away from evil and do good;

so shall you dwell forever." (Psalm 37:9-11, 16, 22, 27)

Again, to the oppressed Jewish faithful of Jesus' day, this is the Good News of the Messiah to come, now evident in the Person and work of Jesus.[1] From a broader perspective, Jesus is talking about a deep satisfaction with what God has given you, a satisfaction or contentment and enjoyment with what God has given, trusting him for everything you need or want.

There is, indeed, a future reference here as well to the time when there will be "new heavens and a new earth" in which the righteous reign with the resurrected Christ. The "kingdom of God" will then be inherited by believers — "You have made them to be a kingdom and priests to serve our God, and they will reign on the earth." (Revelation 5:10)

The Message Bible has it right — "You're blessed when you're content with just who you are—no more, no less. That's the moment you find yourselves proud owners of everything that can't be bought." (Matthew 5:5) Meekness or gentleness is what we can call "practical humility."

How do we get there from here? What are some practical ways to realize the truth of this beatitude in your personal life today? Here are some markers to consider. First, we must see gentleness and humility as "beautiful" — not weakness, or something to be avoided, or something that is just personality based.

Second, examine what modern leadership teachers call your "character wake." Everyone leaves a wake behind them, much like a big ship in the ocean. What is in your "wake" as a person? What do people see and value about you? What do they remember about you? What will they say about you at your gravesite? Will they say he or she was a man or woman of gentleness?

Third, practice three character strengths that will help produce this kind of gentleness and humility — Be approachable; Be sensitive; Be teachable.

Finally, foster a "culture of humility" around yourself and others, what Bill Hybels from Willow Creek Church called "impression management." Watch the way you interact with others. Look at your body language— is it communicating pride and self-congratulation, or gentleness and humility? Learn to be secure in yourself and with what God has given you and gifted you to be. Establish a culture at work and school that resists arrogance. Have an inner circle of friends to help you deal with your pride.

"Kingdom people are not sectarians protesting the larger society just for the sake of being different. Kingdom values, rooted in the deep love and abiding grace of God, seed new ways of thinking and living."[2]

Self Reflection & Discussion

1. How do you look at "gentleness" or "meekness?" Is this a desirable trait for you?
2. Describe your present "character wake." Does it exude "meekness?"
3. Of the three qualities of being approachable, sensitive and teachable, with what quality do you most struggle? Why?
4. How is your "impression management" at work or at school? Does it speak of gentleness and meekness?

Notes

1. "The Hebrew word underlying πραεῖς is עֲנָוִים the same word that occurs in Isa 61:1, which the LXX there translates πτωχοί, "poor." Therefore we have approximately the same thought here as in the first beatitude. In view are not persons who are submissive, mild, and unassertive, but those who are humble in the sense of being oppressed (hence, "have been humbled"), bent over by the injustice of the ungodly, but who are soon to realize their reward. Those in such a condition have no recourse but to depend upon God." (Donald A. Hagner, *Matthew 1–13, Word Biblical Commentary*, Vol 33A, Bruce M. Metzger (Editor), David Allen Hubbard (Editor), Glenn W. Barker (Editor), John D. W. Watts (Series Editor), James W. Watts (Series Editor), Ralph P. Martin (Series Editor), Lynn Allan Losie (Series Editor) (Zondervan, 2015), 92ff.)
2. Donald B. Kraybill, *The Upside Down Kingdom* (Herald Press, 2011 Update).

An Appetite For God

The Fourth Beatitude

"Blessed are those who hunger and thirst for righteousness,
for they shall be satisfied."
"Blessed are those who hunger and thirst for righteousness,
for they will be filled."
"You're blessed when you've worked up a good appetite for God.
He's food and drink in the best meal you'll ever eat."
(Matthew 5:6 ESV, NIV & KJV, The Message)

Committed, but not close. Convinced, but not compelled. I believe this would be the honest state of many believers today. They affirm the Person and work of Jesus Christ. They adhere to the written Word of God. They practice their faith regularly and attend church and other religious activities consistently. Many have become active members of Christian churches and ministries.

Yet, something seems to be missing. Their enthusiasm and zeal for God seems to be lagging. A "panting after God" (Psalm 42:1) is foreign to their faith journeys. A "hunger and thirst for righteousness" has been dumbed down to a conventional desire for the same. We want to be righteous. We want to be "satisfied" with God and our faith. We desire the right things, but have failed to pursue them with the hunger and thirst that should describe our desires. We don't believe or feel we need such an ardent and passionate desire for God. Or, we have lost that desire in the busyness of life and the normality of belief.

Jesus is speaking in this fourth beatitude to the "literally hungry and thirsty, i.e., the downtrodden and oppressed, who especially hunger and thirst after the justice associated with the coming of God's eschatological rule. . . . The poor, the grieving, and the downtrodden (i.e., those who have experienced injustice) are by definition those who long for God to act. They are the righteous who will inherit the kingdom."[1] Yet, the scope of this beatitude goes beyond those faithfully waiting Jewish poor and oppressed to the spiritually needy of our day and age. He is speaking about real spiritual hunger and thirst.

Spiritual hunger shows us the true character of a godly person — He hungers and thirsts after spiritual things (Isaiah 26:9; Psalm 73:25). A true saint is carried upon the wing of desire. It is the very temper and constitution of a gracious soul to thirst after God (Psalm 42:2). In the word preached, how he is big with desire! These are some of the pantings of his soul: 'Lord, you have led me into your courts. O that I may have your sweet presence, that your glory may fill the temple! Will you draw some sacred lineaments of grace upon my soul that I may be more assimilated and changed into the likeness of my dear Savior?' In prayer, how is the soul filled with passionate longings after Christ! Prayer is expressed by 'unutterable groans' (Romans 8:26). The heart sends up whole volleys of sighs to heaven, 'Lord, one beam of your love! Lord, one drop of your blood!'[2]

Perhaps this is too emotional for most of us, too subjective, too mystical for us to grasp and feel. Thomas Watson points to a number of reasons why such spiritual hunger and thirst is lacking among even religiously minded people.[3] Lack of hunger and thirst is because people have never felt any emptiness of soul. They have given a nod to Jesus, perhaps have attended a church membership or baptism class, but have never really needed Christ. They have proceeded on the argument that it is the "right thing to do," but have never felt it is the most desperately needed thing to do.

Lack of hunger and thirst is due to the thought that I can get along quite well with God without it — "Grace is a commodity that is least missed. You shall hear men complain they lack health, they lack trading—but never complain they lack righteousness."[4] They would rather spiritually sleep, or look for what Watson called "elegance and notion" in preaching, intellectual stimulation that never bothers the conscience and goes no deeper than the Sunday sermon.

Lack of spiritual hunger and thirst is due to a preference for other worldly pursuits. Every Sunday morning I pass a soccer field filled with cars and people of all ages watching or playing games of soccer rather than attending the church which is right beside their fields. Perhaps this is judgmental, but it is a current demonstration that even family-minded people today choose other activities besides the worship and desire of God in their lives and priorities.

Commentators point to Psalm 107 as the Old Testament backdrop to the reference to the "hungry and thirsty" —

> . . . the psalmist writes, "Then they cried to the LORD in their trouble, and he delivered them from their distress" (v 6), and then a few verses later continues, "For he satisfies the thirsty and the hungry he fills with good things" (v 9), where the LXX [Septuagint] contains the same verb χορτάζειν, "to fill," as in Matthew. This is the language of messianic fulfillment: he has filled the hungry soul with good things (cf Luke 1:53). It is the language of those who at long last have been "redeemed from trouble" (cf Ps 107:2; for a similar sense of "thirsting" for salvation, cf Pss 42:1–3; 63:1).[5]

The "righteousness" those who hunger and thirst seek could be final justice from the King of righteousness for God's people. It could also be personal righteousness, a right way of thinking and living for God.

A notable Psalm on such hungering and thirsting after God is Psalm 63. Most believe this is a personal Psalm penned by the historical King David (cf. v. 11). The scene is in the wilderness or wasteland of southern Judah. This was the second desert experience for David, the first being while he was fleeing from King Saul (cf. 1 Samuel 23:14–15; 24:1). The reference is from the rebellion of Absalom when David was forced from the throne for a time (cf. 2 Samuel 15:23–30).

Note the painful weariness — "O God, you are my God; earnestly I seek you; my soul thirsts for you; my flesh faints for you, as in a dry and weary land where there is no water." (Ps. 63:1) The Puritan writers all point to the necessary pain of spiritual deprivation that generates such hunger and thirst for God. Such painful necessity has been lacking in modern Christianity for some time. This time for David was a draining, difficult and agonizing experience for him when his throne was illegally usurped by his own son, Absalom. This Psalm is a reminder of how we are to deal with injustice and the emotional and spiritual pressure it brings to our lives. It forms a suitable backdrop to this fourth beatitude. I believe we can outline what spiritual hunger and thirst look like from such a Psalm.

God becomes *my desire* (cf. Ps. 63:1–4). God to David and every spiritually hungry and thirsty person after him is not a distant Deity, not a theological point, not a random search on the internet. He has to become "my God," a personal God with whom I have a personal son or daughter relationship — "But I am not ashamed, for I know whom I have believed, and I am convinced that he is able to guard until that day what has been entrusted to me." (2 Timothy 1:12)

Notice his intimacy with this God. He seeks God "earnestly" (or "early" at dawn [KJV]). He "thirsts" for God. He "longs" for God. He remembers happier days when he "saw" God with the inward eye of worship" — "For the LORD is righteous; he loves righteous deeds; the upright shall behold his face." "One thing have I asked of the LORD, that will I seek after: that I may dwell in the house of the LORD all the days of my life, to gaze upon the beauty of the LORD and to inquire in his temple." (Ps. 11:7; 27:4) God's "love" is better than "life" — "For to me to live is Christ, and to die is gain." (Phil. 1:21) He engages in "open handed" posture of prayer — "So I will bless you as long as I live; in your name I will lift up my hands ["palms" in Hebrew]." "Then Solomon stood before the altar of the LORD in the presence of all the assembly of Israel and spread out his hands toward heaven." "I desire then that in every place the men should pray, lifting holy hands without anger or quarreling." (Ps. 63:4; 1 Kings 8:22; 1 Tim. 2:8)

Secondly, God becomes my *delight* (cf. Ps. 63:5–8). The "satisfaction" God promises to those who hunger and thirst after righteousness is a "feasting" of the soul in contrast to the leanness of the wilderness in our lives — "My soul will be satisfied as with fat and rich food." (Ps. 63:5a) This is what Jesus himself noted in response to the Devil in the temptation in the wilderness of his day, and what He said to his disciples — "And the tempter came and said to him, "If you are the Son of God, command these stones to become loaves of bread." But he answered, "It is written, "'Man shall not live by bread alone, but by every word that comes from the mouth of God.'" "Meanwhile the disciples were urging him, saying, "Rabbi, eat." But he said to them, "I have food to eat that you do not know about." So the disciples said to one another, "Has anyone brought him something to eat?" Jesus said to them, "My food is to do the will of him who sent me and to accomplish his work." (Matthew 4:3, 4; John 4:31–34)

Exhuberant shouts of *full-throated praise* come from those who hunger and thirst after God — "I wake the echoes" (Ps. 63:5 [NEB]). They experience *peace* during the night hours, the "watches of the night." (Ps. 63:6) They dwell in the "shadow of God's wings" (Ps. 63:7), experiencing the *parental shelter of God himself*. And they are encouraged to persevere in such close communion with God — "my soul clings (or "cleaves" or "sticks") to you." (Ps. 63:8) — "Therefore a man shall leave his father and his mother and *hold fast* to his wife, and they shall become one flesh." "Then they lifted up their voices and wept again. And Orpah kissed her mother-in-law, but Ruth *clung* to her." (Genesis 2:24; Ruth 1:14)

For those who hunger and thirst after God's righteousness, God is their *defense* (cf. Ps. 63:9–11). God is a God of final justice — "But those who seek to destroy my life shall go down into the depths of the earth; they shall be given over to the power of the sword; they shall be a portion for jackals." "Or do you presume on the riches of his kindness and forbearance and patience, not knowing that God's kindness is meant to lead you to repentance? But because of your hard and impenitent heart you are storing up wrath for yourself on the day of wrath when God's righteous judgment will be revealed. He will render to each one according to his works." (Ps. 63:9, 10; Romans 2:4–6)

David here reasserts his divine calling as "king" even though he is currently and unjustly banished from the throne — "But the king shall rejoice in God; all who swear by him shall exult, for the mouths of liars will be stopped." "Of whom the world was not worthy—wandering about in deserts and mountains, and in dens and caves of the earth." "And from

Jesus Christ the faithful witness, the firstborn of the dead, and the ruler of kings on earth. To him who loves us and has freed us from our sins by his blood and made us a kingdom, priests to his God and Father, to him be glory and dominion forever and ever. Amen." (Ps. 63:11; Heb. 11:38; Rev. 1:5, 6) For those who hunger and thirst after righteousness, they will be finally and fully satisfied. Justice will finally prevail in the kingdom of God. What is only now partially revealed will be fully revealed when Jesus the King returns. This is the hope of the faithful, of those who hunger and thirst after righteousness.

How does a person foster spiritual hunger and thirst? [SEE Appendix here also.] Watson gives some practical advice here. First, avoid those things that hinder one's appetite for God. The Psalmist pleads, "Turn my eyes from looking at worthless things; and give me life in your ways." Or, as *The Message* puts it, "Divert my eyes from toys and trinkets, invigorate me on the pilgrim way." (Psalm 119:37) On what we focus our attention is what captivates and seizes us. As Watson so quaintly says, "These windy vapors spoil the appetite."[6]

Nourish your spiritual appetite — "Sauce whets and sharpens the appetite. There is a twofold sauce which provokes holy appetite: first, the 'bitter herbs' of repentance. He who tastes gall and vinegar in sin, hungers after the body and blood of the Lord. Second, affliction. God often gives us this sauce to sharpen our hunger after grace."[7] We need to practice what is called "dynamic repentance," turning from sin and turning to God everyday. Repentance is not just a once-for-all remedy for all sins. When you fail God, when you miss God's mark, when you sin . . . repent.

Make such spiritual hunger and thirst a *normal* part of Christian living. We need to get over the thinking that such hungering and thirsting is special, or only for the spiritual elite. We need to sing again and again that wonderful ancient Irish hymn, "Be Thou My Vision" —

> Be Thou my vision, O Lord of my heart;
> Naught be all else to me, save that Thou art;
> Thou my best thought, by day or by night;
> Waking or sleeping, Thy presence my light.

44

Be Thou my wisdom, and Thou my true Word;
I ever with Thee and Thou with me, Lord;
Thou my great Father and I, Thy true son;
Thou in me dwelling, and I with Thee one.

Riches I heed not, nor man's empty praise;
Thou mine inheritance, now and always;
Thou and Thou only, first in my heart;
O King of glory, my treasure Thou art.

O King of glory, my victory won;
Rule and reign in me 'til Thy will be done;
Heart of my own heart, whatever befall;
Still be my vision, O Ruler of all.[8]

Self Reflection & Discussion

1. Why is spiritual hunger and thirst so missing from the modern church?
2. Read through Psalm 63 several times. What parts of this Psalm resonate with you and your spiritual journey?
3. Are you "satisfied" with God? Elaborate.

Notes

1. Donald Hagner, *Matthew 1–13, Word Biblical Commentary*, Vol. 33A (Zondervan, 2015), 95.
2. Thomas Watson, "Spiritual Hunger," *The Beatitudes: An Exposition of Matthew 5:1-12*, 1660, Monergism eBook, https://www.monergism.com/topics/free-ebooks.
3. *Ibid.*
4. *Ibid.*
5. Hagner.
6. Watson, "Spiritual Hunger," *The Beatitudes.*
7. *Ibid.*
8. Dallan Forgaill (530-598), translated by Mary Elizabeth Byrne (1880-1931), adapted by Eleanor Henrietta Hull (1860-1935).

"Carefull" Christianity
The Fifth Beatitude

"Blessed are the merciful, for they shall receive mercy."
"You're blessed when you care. At the moment of being 'carefull,'
you find yourselves cared for."
(Mathew 5:7 ESV, NIV, KJV, The Message)

D
r. Tim Kimmel from Family Matters Ministry has described
Christianity as practiced today in many places as one of six
unfortunate lifestyles.[1] "Compulsory" Christianity is where
the second and third generations of Christians attend the churches of
their forefathers out of compulsion, being forced to act like Christians.
"Cliché" Christianity is a religion where the words are there, the songs are
sung, and the churches are filled with the "same old/same old" trappings.

"Comfortable" Christianity is that state of mind and practice where
our belief systems remain unchallenged, where Christians live within
themselves, where the lack of nonChristian friends is evident. Could you,
for instance, name five *close nonChristian* friends in your life? "Cocoon"
Christianity is a faith that has an unrealistic view of the world system
around them, where they are overly critical of other Christians and other
churches, and where they studiously seek to hide from modern reality.
"Copycat" Christianity is where faith is mimicked instead of being made
personal and transformational. "Country Club" Christianity is where
social programs and agendas have replaced Bible based themes and
teaching.

It is only *Christ-empowered Christianity* that is the real thing,
that demonstrates the lifestyle of the fifth beatitude. What is Christ-
empowered Christianity? It is a Christianity that has the same heart and
practice as its founder, Jesus Christ. That practice is showing "mercy." The

God we serve is a God "rich in mercy" (Ephesians 2:4), a God who saves us "according to his own mercy" (Titus 3:5; 1 Peter 1:13), a God who invites us to pray because He is full of mercy (Hebrews 4:16). This God abounding in mercy and grace wants us to show mercy, to be "carefull" of others, as *The Message* puts it in Matthew 5:7.

Thayer will define "mercy" as "kindness or good will toward the miserable and afflicted, joined with a desire to relieve them."[2] Robertson says "mercy" is "a self-acting law of the moral world."[3] "Mercy" has been described as "God not giving us what we deserve." And, so, showing mercy is not dependent on the object, but rather on our own spiritual state.

What does it mean to show "mercy" or be "merciful?" Matthew gives us the model of Jesus to follow — "When he saw the crowds, he had compassion for them, because they were harassed and helpless, like sheep without a shepherd." (Matt. 9:36) Jesus tells us and shows us that being merciful requires, first of all, that we *open our eyes*! When Jesus saw the crowds of his day, he did not see criminals, con-artists, addicts, alcoholics, prostitudes, liars, cheats or misfits. He saw "harrassed" and "helpless" people made in the image of God his Father. He saw people as "skinned,"[4] flayed, troubled, annoyed, fractured and exhausted by their Pharisaic rulers. He saw people helpless, neglected, forsaken and littered like corpses scattered on a field of battle.

What do we see when we look around at our neighbors, unsaved family members, when we shop at our favorite stores, fill our gas tanks at the corner market, when we turn on the TV set, or go to the movies, or see a video conference on our smart devices? Part of the reason why the New Testament church turned their world upside down was that they saw their world through the eyes of Jesus. Do we? Do you?

People are a lot like eggs. They all look pretty much the same on the outside, different sizes perhaps, but similar oval shapes, similar hard shells. We might assume the insides are all the same. But, like eggs, some are raw inside. Some are soft-boiled inside, and some are hard-boiled inside. And we never really see an egg until we look inside the shell. Opening our eyes means translating how people, especially Millennials,[5] communicate —

DITYID

NALOPKT

NE1?

WWSD

Do you know what these cryptic letters mean and convey?

Did I tell you I'm distressed?

Not a lot of people know that.

Anyone?

What would Satan do?

And, by the way, texting in LARGE LETTERS means shouting at you! To be merciful means, first of all, to open our eyes to our world as seen by Jesus.

To be merciful, in the second place, is to *open our hearts* to the people we really see. Instead of turning away from the people Jesus saw as recorded in Matthew 9, He had "compassion" on them, individually and collectively. The term the Gospel writers use usually means "to pity," but it really conveys much more than a "sorry feeling" about others. "Compassion" is a "sensitive alertness that drives us outside of ourselves to look beyond the hard-shelled exterior to the real-life needs of people around us."[6] Jesus was much more than merely courteous, or civil, or even tolerant of people. He actually cared for them — enough to die on a rugged cross for such people.

As Jesus sends out the twelve disciples in Matthew 10, he tells them to exercise "sensitive alertness." As Jesus sends us out through the Great Commission (Matthew 28:19, 20), he tells us to engage people with "sensitive alertness." Yes, we acknowledge people without God as sinners, as "harrassed and helpless," as "without God and without hope in this world." But we see them through hearts of mercy and love.

Third, being merciful means we must *open our hands* — "And proclaim as you go, saying, 'The kingdom of heaven is at hand.' Heal the sick, raise the dead, cleanse lepers, cast out demons. You received without paying; give without pay." (Matt. 10:7, 8) We are to use our God-given gifts and talents and treasure to bestow on others and bless others.

Instead of being *consumers*, we need to become *givers*. Instead of acquiring more and more, we need to give more and more. Howard Hendricks once said,

> Why don't I want to get involved with that woman or girl or man? Why don't I want to get involved with that obnoxious kid? because it's not comfortable. It's going to cost me. That was the problem on the Samaritan road with the priest and Levite (cf. Luke 10). They see a sign, "Danger! Mess ahead!" They detour, and the guy who is not supposed to be giving is the guy who pays the whole freight. 'Freely you have received; freely give.' God never asks you to give anything to him until he informs you of what he has given you. When you understand what you have in Jesus Christ, you are in debt up to your eyeballs for the rest of your life.[7]

The denomination in which I am affiliated has ten core values or ten commitment principles which guide the churches and ministries of the denomination. Two of of those ten core values state, "We serve compassionately — We value serving others at their point of need, following the example of our Lord Jesus," and, "We live simply — We value uncluttered lives, which free us to love boldly, give generously, and serve joyfully."[8] Love boldly, give generously and serve joyfully. These seem to sum up the fifth beatitude.

What does God want from Christians who seek to live out this beatitude? God wants an attitude that matches Jesus and was evidenced in the early church and its leaders. John Maxwell has well said, "Your attitude determines your altitude" in life. This is an attitude that Paul had when in prison for the cause of Christ, he prayed not for his release or comfort or needs, but rather for those around him. He prayed that he could proclaim Jesus to them clearly and convincingly — "At the same time, pray also for us, that God may open to us a door for the word, to declare the mystery of Christ, on account of which I am in prison—that I may make it clear, which is how I ought to speak." (Colossians 4:3, 4)

A merciful attitude and lifestyle says people are reachable, that obstacles are conquerable. A merciful attitude and life chooses to focus on the positive sketches of the image of God in people. A merciful attitude and life resists Satan's urges to see the negative in others. A life and attitude such as this receives this blessing — "they shall obtain mercy." Thomas Watson notes the blessings a merciful person receives in this life —

In his person: 'Blessed is he who considers the poor' (Psalm 41:1). Let him go where he will, a blessing goes along with him. He is in favor with God. God casts a smiling aspect upon him.

Blessed in his name: 'He shall be had in everlasting remembrance' (Psalm 112:6). When the niggard's name shall rot, the name of a merciful man shall be embalmed with honor, and give forth its scent as the wine of Lebanon.

Blessed in his estate: 'He shall abound in all things'. 'The liberal soul shall be made fat' (Proverbs 2:25). He shall have the fat of the earth and the dew of heaven. He shall not only have the venison—but the blessing.

Blessed in his posterity: 'He is ever merciful and lends; and his seed is blessed' (Psalm 37:26). He shall not only leave an estate behind—but a blessing behind to his children, and God will see that the entail of that blessing shall not be cut off.

Blessed in his negotiations: 'For this thing the Lord your God shall bless you in all your works, and in all that you put your hand unto' (Deuteronomy 15:10). The merciful man shall be blessed in his building, planting, journeying. Whatever he is about, a blessing shall empty itself upon him. 'Wherever he treads there shall be a rose'. He shall be a prosperous man. The honeycomb of a blessing shall be still dropping upon him.

Blessed with long life: 'The Lord will preserve him and keep him alive' (Psalm 41:2). He has helped to keep others alive, and God will keep him alive. Is there anything then, lost by mercifulness? It spins out the silver thread of life. Many are taken away the sooner for their unmercifulness. Because their hearts are straitened, their lives are shortened.[9]

Self Reflection & Discussion

1. Are you a "carefull" Christian? Prove it.

2. When you think of giving mercy, what images come to mind?

3. Describe the mercies you have received from others.

Notes

1. Dr. Tim Kimmel, *Family Matters Ministry*, https://familymatters.net/about/tim-kimmel/.

2. Joseph Henry Thayer, *Thayer's Greek–English Lexicon of the New Testament*, 1885, digitized by https://www.accordancebible.com.

3. Archibald Thomas Robertson, *Word Pictures in the New Testament*, Vol 1, The Gospel According to Matthew and The Gospel According to Mark. digitized by https://www.accordancebible.com.

4. "Harrassed," with the Greek being ἐσκυλμένοι.

5. "Millennials, also known as Generation Y or Gen Y, are the demographic cohort following Generation X and preceding Generation Z. Demographers and researchers typically use the early 1980s as starting birth years and the mid-1990s to early 2000s as ending birth years. Millennials are sometimes referred to as "echo boomers" due to a major surge in birth rates in the 1980s and 1990s, and because millennials are often the children of the baby boomers." (https://en.wikipedia.org/wiki/Millennials)

6. "*Compassion* literally means "to suffer together." Among emotion researchers, it is defined as the feeling that arises when you are confronted with another's suffering and feel motivated to relieve that suffering. Compassion is not the same as empathy or altruism, though the concepts are related." (https://greatergood.berkeley.edu/topic/compassion/definition)

7. "Howard George Hendricks (April 5, 1924 – February 20, 2013). For over fifty years, Howard G. Hendricks was a professor at Dallas Theological Seminary, where he taught "Bible Exposition and Hermeneutics" to freshmen. He mentored many Christian leaders, including Chuck Swindoll, Tony Evans, Joseph Stowell and David Jeremiah. He was a keynote speaker for Promise Keepers and authored sixteen books. He ministered in over 80 countries, and he also served as chaplain for the Dallas Cowboys football team from 1976 to 1984." (https://en.wikipedia.org/wiki/Howard_Hendricks)

8. The Brethren in Christ Church produced ten "core values" of their denominational faith perspective. They can be found at https://bicus.org/about/what-we-believe/core-values/.

9. Thomas Watson. "A Discourse of Mercifulness," *The Beatitudes: An Exposition of Matthew 5:1-12*, 1660, Monergism eBook, https://www.monergism.com/topics/free-ebooks.

Gospel Integrity
The Sixth Beatitude

"Blessed are the pure in heart, for they shall see God."
"You're blessed when you get your inside world—your mind and heart—
put right. Then you can see God in the outside world."
(Mathew 5:8 ESV, NIV, KJV, The Message)

Integrity. We usually think of integrity as a person keeping their word, or not cheating on taxes, or not pilfering a company's money or products. These are indeed outward signs of integrity, but as Henry Cloud pointed out in his book, *Integrity: The Courage To Meet The Demand of Reality*, integrity deals with much more than good ethics or good business practices. It deals with what we would call "personhood" — "While character includes our usual understanding of ethics and integrity, it is much more than that as well. Another way of putting it is that ethical functioning is a part of character, but not all of it."[1]

Jesus put it this way — "But what comes out of the mouth proceeds from the heart, and this defiles a person. For out of the heart come evil thoughts, murder, adultery, sexual immorality, theft, false witness, slander. These are what defile a person. But to eat with unwashed hands does not defile anyone." (Matthew 15:18–20) He was correcting a Pharisaic understanding of uncleanness, that lack of ceremonial washing of the hands before one eats is a mark of being unclean before God. A person is defined by their "inside world," not by their external habits. And, external habits flow from their inside world.

Donald Hagner in the *Word Biblical Commentary* sees this beatitude paralleling Psalm 24:3, 4 — "Who shall ascend the hill of the LORD? And who shall stand in his holy place? He who has clean hands and a pure heart, who does not lift up his soul to what is false and does not swear deceitfully." "'Pure in heart' refers to the condition of the inner core of a person, that is, to thoughts and motivation, and hence anticipates the internalizing of the commandments by Jesus in the material that follows in the sermon. It takes for granted right actions but asks for integrity in the doing of those actions, i.e., a consistency between the inner springs of one's conduct and the conduct itself."[2]

Gospel integrity is a consistency between what is inside a person and the conduct of that person. The Puritan, Thomas Watson, calls it "evangelical purity; whence grace is mingled with some sin—like gold in the ore; like wine which has a dreg in it; like fine cloth with a blemish; like Nebuchadnezzar's image, part of silver, and part of clay (Daniel 2:35). This mixture God calls purity in a gospel-sense; as a face may be said to be fair, which has some freckles in it. Where there is a study of purity and a loathing ourselves for our impurity—this is to be 'pure in heart.'"[3] He goes on to distinguish purity of heart from external morality —

If we must be pure in heart—then we must not rest in outward purity. Morality is not sufficient. A swine may be washed—yet a swine still. Morality does but wash a man, grace changes him. Morality may shine in the eyes of the world—but it differs as much from purity, as a pebble differs from the diamond. Morality is but strewing flowers on a dead corpse. A man who is but highly moral—is but a tame devil. How many have made 'morality' their Savior! Morality will damn, as well as heinous vice. A boat may be sunk with gold, as well as with dung.[4]

The goal of purity of heart is consistency between who a person is and what a person does. "Purity here is to be taken in a larger sense for the several kinds and degrees of holiness. They are said to be pure, who are consecrated people, having the oil of grace poured upon them."[5] "Pure in heart" people are not sinless people, but are people striving for holiness of heart and life before God. What does such consistency look like?

Psalm 15 talks about people of consistent purity of heart who are able to stand in the presence of God, to worship God in spirit and in truth —

O LORD, who shall sojourn in your tent?
Who shall dwell on your holy hill?

He who walks blamelessly and does what is right
and speaks truth in his heart;
who does not slander with his tongue
and does no evil to his neighbor,
nor takes up a reproach against his friend;
in whose eyes a vile person is despised,
but who honors those who fear the LORD;
who swears to his own hurt and does not change;
who does not put out his money at interest
and does not take a bribe against the innocent.
He who does these things shall never be moved.
(Psalm 15:1–5)

"O LORD, who shall sojourn in your tent? Who shall dwell on your holy hill?" (Psalm 15:1) The "holy hill" refers to the spiritual dwelling place of God. This is the promise of Jesus to those who are pure of heart — "they shall see God."

It is to be noted that a "blameless" walk in Psalm 15 does not mean a sinless walk, or a perfect walk, but a lifestyle where no charge from the outside world against you can stick. This "blameless" walk and all the other exterior moral qualities mentioned in the Psalm come from "speaking truth in his heart." The heart reference is key to all the qualities outlined in the Psalm. A "blameless" person is a person of consistent integrity — "I have done what is just and right; do not leave me to my oppressors." (Psalm 119:121) "If you know that he is righteous, you may be sure that everyone who practices righteousness has been born of him." (1 John 2:29) "Little children, let no one deceive you. Whoever practices righteousness is righteous, as he is righteous." (1 John 3:7) "By this it is evident who are the children of God, and who are the children of the devil: whoever does not practice righteousness is not of God, nor is the one who does not love his brother." (1 John 3:10)

A person of consistent integrity has a right relationship with his neighbor (Psalm 15:3–5). Jesus in the Great Commandment put it this way — "Jesus answered, "The most important is, 'Hear, O Israel: The Lord our God, the Lord is one. And you shall love the Lord your God with all your heart and with all your soul and with all your mind and with all your strength.' The second is this: 'You shall love your neighbor as yourself.' There is no other commandment greater than these." (Mark 12:29–31) The commandment to love our neighbor takes on the same importance as our love of God, and such love must come from "all your heart."

This means no slander and no practice that would harm your neighbor, like gossip (cf. Leviticus 5:4; 1 Peter 3:8). This also means no taking advantage of others through dishonest business practices, like unreasonable interest or bribery (Psalm 15:5). The "pure in heart" person loves what God loves, and hates what God hates. His inner motives and outward life reflect the character and priorities of the Lord.

Another way of talking about purity of heart is the character quality of "singlemindedness" — "Draw near to God, and he will draw near to you. Cleanse your hands, you sinners, and *purify your hearts,* you double-minded." (James 4:8) A "double-minded" person has a double standard. "The reader who is double-minded seeks to be friendly with the world and with God (4:4). But such double allegiance is impossible. To befriend the world (i.e., resort to worldly methods to bring in the kingdom) is to oppose God and his way."[6] James connects inward disposition with outward practices.

> The sincere Christian serves God with the 'whole heart' (Psalm 119:2). Hypocrites have a double heart (Psalm 12:2)—a heart for God, and a heart for sin. 'Their heart is divided' (Hosea 10:2). God loves a broken heart—but not a divided heart. An upright heart is a whole heart. The full stream and torrent of the affections runs out after God. A sincere heart 'follows God fully' (Numbers 14:24).[7]

Again, "singlemindedness" is a matter of the heart and is a quality of the pure in heart. The reward is to be able to "draw near to God" — "It is possible that the thought of drawing near to God is reminiscent of the OT idea of a priest or of Moses coming near to Yahweh (Exod 19:22; 24:2; Deut 16:16; cf Heb 4:16; 7:19)."[8] Consequently, the pure in heart "shall see God."

Purity of heart and purity of conscience are closely related in the

Pastoral Letters as well[9] — "The aim of our charge is love that issues from a pure heart and a good conscience and a sincere faith." (1 Timothy 1:5) "They must hold the mystery of the faith with a clear conscience." (1 Tim. 3:9) "I thank God whom I serve, as did my ancestors, with a clear conscience, as I remember you constantly in my prayers night and day." (2 Tim. 1:3) "So flee youthful passions and pursue righteousness, faith, love, and peace, along with those who call on the Lord from a pure heart." (2 Tim. 2:22) "Having purified your souls by your obedience to the truth for a sincere brotherly love, love one another earnestly from a pure heart." (1 Peter 1:22) "A man of sincere heart, dares not act in the least against his conscience. He is the most magnanimous—yet the most cautious. He is bold in suffering (Proverbs 28:1) but fearful of sin (Genesis 39:9). He dares not get an estate by sinful shifts, or rise upon the ruins of another."[10]

How does a person get a "pure heart?" You get a pure heart by loving and absorbing the Word of God — "Already you are clean because of the word that I have spoken to you." (John 15:3) "Sanctify them in the truth; your word is truth." (John 17:17) Studying the Word of God, and, more importantly, meditating on that Word, will have a cleansing effect on your life and your heart.

Make sure of your relationship with Jesus Christ. "If we say we have no sin, we deceive ourselves, and the truth is not in us. If we confess our sins, he is faithful and just to forgive us our sins and to cleanse us from all unrighteousness." (1 John 1:8, 9) The old Puritans called this a "bath for the soul." Have you bathed your soul in the blood of Christ? Have you gone to Christ as your only righteousness?

Be careful of close associations with those whose hearts are not pure, whose hearts evidence corruptible behavior by their daily lives.

If you would be pure, walk with those who are pure. As the communion of the saints is in our Creed, so it should be in our company. 'He who walks with the wise, shall be wise' (Proverbs 13:20), and he who walks with the pure, shall be pure. The saints are like a bed of spices. By intermixing ourselves with them we shall partake of their savouriness. Association begets assimilation.[11]

Self Reflection & Discussion

1. How do you define or describe "integrity?"
2. Why is *consistency* in integrity so crucial to having a pure heart?
3. What does it mean to "see God?"
4. Go through Psalm 15 and rate yourself on the character qualities described there. In what do you need to improve?

Notes

1. Henry Cloud, *Integrity: The Courage to Meet the Demands of Reality* (HarperBusiness, 2006), 8.
2. Donald Hagner, *Matthew 1–13, Word Biblical Commentary*, Vol. 33A (Zondervan, 2015), 95. "The sixth beatitude bears strong similarity to the thought of Ps 24[LXX: 23]:3–4, where the LXX [Septuagint] refers, as does the present text, to the καθαρὸς τῇ καρδία, "the pure in heart" (cf Pss 51:10; 73:1; linked here with "guiltless hands"), who will go up to the mountain of the Lord and stand in his holy place."
3. Thomas Watson. "Heart Purity," *The Beatitudes: An Exposition of Matthew 5:1-12*, 1660, Monergism eBook, https://www.monergism.com/topics/free-ebooks.
4. *Ibid.*
5. *Ibid.*
6. Hagner, 95.
7. Watson, "Heart Purity."
8. Hagner.
9. *Ibid.*
10. Watson.
11. *Ibid.*

God's Peace Corps
The Seventh Beatitude

"Blessed are the peacemakers, for they shall be called sons
[children] of God."
"You're blessed when you can show people how to cooperate instead of
compete or fight. That's when you discover who you really are, and your
place in God's family."
(Mathew 5:9 ESV, [NIV, KJV], The Message)

I have a friend, a retired Lieutenant Colonel from the Army War College in Carlisle, PA who told me that the Army War College top brass are much more concerned with peace-making than war -making at the college. Martin Luther King once said, "I refuse to accept the view that mankind is so tragically bound to the starless midnight of racism and war that the bright daybreak of peace and brotherhood can never become a reality . . . I believe that unarmed truth and unconditional love will have the final word."[1]

What is this "peace" that we are to make? Jesus is not just talking about a cease-fire, or a cessation of hostilities, or even a truce between individuals or nations here. He is also not talking about what was called the *pax Romana* of his day, the external peace that Rome had when He gave the Sermon on the Mount.[2] Epictetus, a nonChristian thinker and writer from the first century, put it this way, "While the Emperor may give peace from war on land and sea, he is unable to give peace from passion, grief and envy. He cannot give peace of heart, for which man yearns more than even for outward peace."[3]

Think with me about the audience of Jesus day. These were Jewish people, people schooled and taught and conditioned for only one kind of peace, that is true peace, the "Shalom" peace of the Old Testament. This is not some new concept Jesus teaches the people, but an old truth repackaged and made relevant by the Prince of Peace Himself.

What is this "Shalom" peace? It is "a state and sense of wholeness and well-being applied to individuals, relationships and even cities and nations."[4] This peace that we are instructed to make is a peace with God, and a peace given by God through the Messiah, Jesus Christ. It is a peace in relation to God and to oneself as well as life's circumstances. Psalm 119:165 reminds us — "Great peace have they who love your (God's) law and nothing can make them stumble." David reminds us that stability and safety and firmness in the path of duty comes from an inner right relationship with God, an inner harmony with yourself.

But it's also wider than inner peace. It is a relational peace, a peace among people, a mutual harmony. One writer has put it this way, "As Christ is honored and is given admission to human lives, to that extent the peace on earth, which He came to bring, becomes a glorious actuality. In so far as people live outside of Jesus Christ, the earth remains in a state of disorder and strife without real peace."[5] It was the prophet Isaiah who tells us in our reality TV age that the "wicked are like the tossing sea, which cannot rest, whose waves cast up mire and mud. There is no peace, says my God, for the wicked." (Isaiah 57:20, 21)

People might object and say, "Oh, you're just being too religious when you say that peace between people and nations comes from Jesus Christ." No, I would maintain that is not just a religious declaration. It is a fundamental reality that people and nations miss when they talk about peace. In the prophet Micah 5:4,5, the promised Messiah will "stand and shepherd his flock in the strength of the Lord, in the majesty of the name of the Lord his God. And they will live securely, for then his greatness will reach to the ends of the earth. And he will be their peace."

The Apostle Paul in the New Testament makes the astounding declaration that it is only through Christ and his Cross that true and lasting peace comes — "But now in Christ Jesus you who once were far off have been brought near by the blood of Christ. For he himself is our peace, who has made us both one and has broken down in his flesh the dividing wall of hostility and might reconcile us both to God in one body through the cross, thereby killing the hostility. And he came and preached peace to you who were far off and peace to those who were near. For through him we both have access in one Spirit to the Father." (Ephesians 2:13,14,16-18) The angels' message to the shepherds on a Jewish hillside 2,000 years ago was "Glory to God in the highest, and on earth peace to men on whom his favor rests." (Luke 2:14)

The early witnesses of the resurrection of Jesus were sent out, as we are, with the "good news of peace through Jesus Christ, who is Lord of all." (Acts 10:36) At best and at most, all that humankind can do without Jesus Christ at the center of reconciliation talks is broker a cease fire perhaps, but they can never end the internal anger, hurt, passion and envy among Jews and Arabs or Al Quaida and the world. People need the Lord for real peace. People need us to tell them and plead with them and teach them about the Prince of Peace!

Another objection might be that this is "soft" peace, that this is just being nice toward one another, whether it be in family relationships, work relationships, marriage relationships or national relationships. No, this peace that Jesus is talking about here in the beatitudes is always joined with the concepts of purity and righteousness — "righteousness and peace kiss each other." (Psalm 85:10) "Wisdom from heaven is pure then peace-loving . . ." (James 3:17) "Oh that you had paid attention to my commandments! Then your peace would have been like a river, and your righteousness like the waves of the sea." (Isaiah 48:18) This is strong peace, holistic peace, real peace.

Jesus goes on in this beatitude to say that peacemakers will be "called" (a sovereign, divine word) "sons of God" or "children of God." In other words, peacemakers take on the character of God when they broker peace, whether it be peace in marriages or families or nations. God in the Bible is called the "God of peace" — "What you have learned and received and heard and seen in me—practice these things, and the God of peace will be with you." (Philippians 4:9) "Now may the God of peace himself sanctify you completely, and may your whole spirit and soul and body be kept blameless at the coming of our Lord Jesus Christ." (1 Thessalonians 5:23)— and his people imitate Him and image Him when they are peacemakers.

Every Christian must become a peacemaker. In the midst of arguing about who would be the "greatest" in the kingdom of God, Jesus says, "Have salt in yourselves, and be at peace with one another." (Mark 9:50) And, "salt" in the tradition of the Old Testament was a sign of fellowship and brotherhood.

In Romans 12:18, we read, "If possible, so far as it depends on you, live peaceably with all." Peacemaking means no personal grudges or vengeance is allowed by the Prince of Peace. In 2 Corinthians 13:11, we read, "Finally, brothers,1 rejoice. Aim for restoration, comfort one another, agree with one another, live in peace; and the God of love and peace will be with you." Fellowship and effective witness for Jesus among the Corinthian believers had been marred by factionalism, personal loyalties and the over emphasis of special gifts of the Spirit. They were engaged in foolish, carnal backbiting. They are to end such behavior.

In speaking to the Thessalonians about the end times and seeking to encourage them, Paul writes, "We ask you, brothers, to respect those who labor among you and are over you in the Lord and admonish you, and to esteem them very highly in love because of their work. Be at peace among yourselves. And we urge you, brothers, admonish the idle, encourage the fainthearted, help the weak, be patient with them all." (1 Thessalonians 5:12–14)

In my over twenty years of work with churches as a church health consultant for NCDAmerica, the one glaring weakness that appears over and over again in church health is the failure to maintain and develop what are called "loving relationships." Open disputes, seething anger, hidden agendas to get back at someone mar many churches. For loving relationships to work, Christians must regularly and often affirm and encourage one another. There must be an atmosphere of trust and joy that permeates the fellowship of believers. Relationships with one another need deepened, and conflicts need biblically resolved on a dynamic basis.[6]

How can an ordinary person be a peacemaker? First, know Jesus for *personal* peace. The truth is that without that inner harmony, that inner solution to the natural anger, resentment, paying back tit-for-tat, that we all have deeply embedded in our natural selves, without Jesus as our personal Prince of peace, we will never become what Jesus teaches here.

Follow Jesus for *relational* peace. Jesus came to make us disciples or followers, not just to give a fire escape to heaven or a prescription for inner pain that lasts a short while. We get along with others, we broker peace when we have the Prince of Peace calling the shots. The more you know Jesus and his Word, the more of a peacemaker you become.

Pray to Jesus for *universal* peace. Psalm 122:6 tells us to pray for the peace of Jerusalem. Isaiah 11 tells of a future time when the wolf will lie with the lamb, when the leopard will lie down with the goat, and a little child will lead them. When will this be? "When the earth is full of the knowledge of the Lord as the waters cover the seas."

Volunteer in your area for just and true peace. There are a number of Victim-Offender Reconciliation Programs across the country and in our cities.

The story is told of a man named Giovanni Francesco Bernadone, once a rich and popular Italian youth. He was the life of the party. In fact, his friends once crowned him "King of Revellers." But he had no peace, no real wholeness to his life. Until one day when he met and bowed before a real King. No, it wasn't any of the earthly potentates of his day. It was the Prince of Peace, Jesus Christ.

After meeting Him, Giovanni wrote a poem expressing his new-found love for God and man —

"Lord, make me an instrument of thy peace;
Where there is hatred, let me sow love;
Where there is injury, pardon;
Where there is doubt, faith;
Where there is despair, hope;
Where there is darkness, light; and
Where there is sadness, joy.
For it is in giving that we receive;
It is in pardoning that we are pardoned;
And it is in dying, that we are born to
Eternal life."

Yes, Giovanni Francesco Bernadone became St. Francis of Assisi.

Self Reflection & Discussion

1. Why is peace lacking in our churches and relationships?
2. How can you become a "peace broker" where you live and work and go to school?
3. Examine your own relationships. Are you a peacemaker? Give examples.

Notes

1. Quote by Martin Luther King, Jr., https://www.brainyquote.com/authors/martin_luther_king_jr.

2. "The substantive εἰρηνοποιοί, "peacemakers," of the seventh beatitude occurs only here in the NT (the verb of the same stem occurs in Col 1:20). In the context of the beatitudes, the point would seem to be directed against the Zealots, the Jewish revolutionaries who hoped through violence to bring the kingdom of God. Such means would have been a continual temptation for the downtrodden and oppressed who longed for the kingdom." (Donald Hagner, *Matthew 1–13, Word Biblical Commentary*, Vol. 33A (Zondervan, 2015), 95.)

3. Quoted by Warren W. Wiersbe, *The Wiersbe Bible Commentary* (David C. Cook, 2007), on Luke 2. Also quoted in "The Vintage Advent of Peace," December 6, 2015, *https://www.slideshare.net/deacongodsey/vintage-advent-messagepeace12615*.

4. Cited in https://firm.org.il/learn/the-meaning-of-shalom/.

5. Drew Desilver, "Who's poor in America? 50 years into the 'War on Poverty,' a data portrait," Pew Research Center, January 13, 2014, *http://www.pewresearch.org/fact-tank/2014/01/13/whos-poor-in-america-50-years-into-the-war-on-poverty-a-data-portrait/*.

6. The author is a church health consultant with NCDAmerica (https://ncdamerica.andrews.edu). Of the eight universal health characteristics of a healthy church or ministry, "loving relationships" is a key quality. The formal definition of "loving relationships" in natural church development (NCD) is "Loving relationships are the heart of a healthy, growing church. Jesus said people will know we are his disciples by our love. Practical demonstration of love builds authentic Christian community and brings others into God's kingdom." If you are interested in a church health check, contact the author for a church health profile at *carl@carlshankconsulting.com*.

The Privilege of Persecution
The Eighth Beatitude[1]

"Blessed are those who are persecuted for righteousness' sake, for theirs
is the kingdom of heaven. Blessed are you when others revile you and
persecute you and utter all kinds of evil against you falsely on my account.
Rejoice and be glad, for your reward is great in heaven, for so they
persecuted the prophets who were before you."
""You're blessed when your commitment to God provokes persecution.
The persecution drives you even deeper into God's kingdom.
Not only that—count yourselves blessed every time people put you down
or throw you out or speak lies about you to discredit me. What it means is
that the truth is too close for comfort and they are uncomfortable.
You can be glad when that happens—give a cheer, even!—for though they
don't like it, I do! And all heaven applauds. And know that you are in good
company. My prophets and witnesses have always gotten into this kind of
trouble."
(Mathew 5:10–12 ESV, The Message)

P ersecution. Christians have been facing persecution of various
sorts and intensities ever since the time of Christ. "The blood
of the martyrs is the seed of the Church," wrote Tertullian in
197 AD. Jesus as Lord of the Church writes to the believers in Smyrna, "'I
know your tribulation and your poverty (but you are rich) and the slander
of those who say that they are Jews and are not, but are a synagogue of
Satan. Do not fear what you are about to suffer. Behold, the devil is about
to throw some of you into prison, that you may be tested, and for ten days
you will have tribulation." (Revelation 2:9, 10)[2]

Religious freedom for evangelical Christians is under attack in
America today. For decades, the American Civil Liberties Union
(ACLU), and other radical anti-Christian groups have been on a mission
to eliminate public expression of our nation's faith and heritage. By
influencing the government, filing lawsuits, and spreading the myth of

the so-called "separation of church and state," the opposition has been successful at forcing its agenda on Americans. Their targeted attacks on religious freedom are more serious and widespread than you may realize. In courtrooms and schoolrooms, offices and shops, public buildings and even churches, those who believe in God are increasingly threatened, punished, and silenced.

A second-grade student at a public school in New Jersey was told that she could not sing "Awesome God" in an after-school talent show.

A pastor of a church in Arizona was ordered to stop holding meetings or Bible studies in his private home.

Five Christian men were threatened with arrest for sharing their faith on a public sidewalk in Virginia.

A Christian student at a university in Missouri was threatened with having her degree withheld because she refused to write a letter to the state legislature expressing her support for homosexual adoption.

A pro-life nurse at a hospital in New York was forced to participate in a late-term abortion, even though her workplace had agreed in writing to honor her religious convictions.[3]

We should not be shocked, should we? The disciples hearing the voice of Jesus in this beatitude understood what Jesus meant when He said, "If they persecuted me, they will persecute you also" (John 15:20).

Jesus calls them "happy" who are "persecuted for righteousness sake." Here ἕνεκεν δικαιοσύνης, "on account of righteousness," points to the character of the recipients of the kingdom as it has hitherto been described in the beatitudes. That is, their loyalty to God and his call upon their lives become in turn the cause of their further suffering. To be identified with Jesus and the kingdom is to be in "the way of righteousness" (cf 21:32); hence ἕνεκεν δικαιοσύνης, "on account of righteousness," finds its counterpart in the ἕνεκεν ἐμοῦ, "on account of me" (cf 10:22), of the following verse.[4]

What is to be noted is that this is not persecution for sinful or bad behavior by the Jewish faithful of Jesus' day, nor for such behavior by Christians of our day. Thomas Watson in 1660 pointed out that Jesus is not condoning Christian persecution for bringing it unwisely upon ourselves, or offences or for promoting factionalism —

> When men through rashness run themselves into trouble, it is a
> cross of their own making and not of God's laying upon them.
> . . . When men suffer by the hand of the magistrate for their
> uncleanness, blasphemies etc., these do not suffer persecution—
> but execution. They die not as martyrs—but as malefactors. They
> suffer evil—for being evil. That is not Christian suffering, when
> they suffer, out of sinister respects, to be cried up as head of a
> party, or to keep up a faction. The apostle implies that a man may
> give his body to be burned—yet go to hell (1 Corinthians 13:3).
> Ambitious men may sacrifice their lives to purchase fame. These
> are the devil's martyrs.[5]

Five prominent truths about Christian persecution stand out in what
Jesus teaches here that apply to all true Christians and true churches of
all ages. First, note that persecution comes from real, human foes! Our
tendency is to treat persecution in America today as "spiritual-only." We
read the stories of Daniel and his three friends as a far distant story in
cruder times, or that those who persecute us aren't somehow responsible.
After all, "they" are not doing the persecuting, we say, Satan is persecuting
us. Well, that's true and not true. People persecute people, not some
invisible force!

Persecution is often intense. Polycarp, an early church father, was
burned in Smyrna (cf. Revelation 2:8–11) as a martyr because he refused
to acknowledge Caesar as Lord. Historians even say that Jews who were
forbidden to work on the Sabbath actually gathered wood for the fire that
killed Polycarp. Antipas (Revelation 2:13) was killed for his faith. The
story there was that he was slowly roasted to death in a brazen bull during
the reign of Domitian. In fact, the term for "martyr" replaced the meaning
of the term for "witness" beginning at Pergamum (cf. Rev. 2:13–18). The
Smyrna Christians underwent the vicious, verbal slander of those who
were nominal Jews, supposedly committed to the sanctity of human life.
(v. 9)

In the spring of 2017, my wife and I along with some friends took a
sacred history tour of England and Scotland. What was striking to us were

the many places where Christ followers were burned at the stake for their faith. I was especially moved by the monument to the Covenanters at the Grassmarket in Old Town Edinburgh, Scotland. There, over one hundred Presbyterians were killed for practicing their faith. And in Oxford, initials carved into the pavement mark the spot where Patrick Hamilton, member of the University, was burned at the stake in 1528 at the age of 24. He became the first martyr of the Scottish Reformation. At St. Andrews, we passed the tribute to George Wishart, a Protestant preacher who was also burned at the stake. The Martyrs Monument in St. Andrews, built in 1843, is a reminder of many who gave their lives for the faith.

Persecution, thirdly, is rooted in a real Satan who really hates God! "Behold, the devil is about to throw some of you into prison . . ." (Rev. 2:10) He is the false accuser of the brethren—"And I heard a loud voice in heaven, saying, "Now the salvation and the power and the kingdom of our God and the authority of his Christ have come, for the accuser of our brothers has been thrown down, who accuses them day and night before our God." (Revelation 12:10)

But, you may say, that was then! What do those days have to do with today? Paul registers a blanket statement description in 2 Timothy 3:1–5 when he uses the words "in the last days," which most everyone agrees is that time period from the death and resurrection of Jesus to his Second Coming. These are our days! Why tell us what many of us, including Timothy, already know? The Apostle wants to emphasize that opposition to God's truth and God's ways is not a passing situation, but rather a permanent characteristic of the last days! These will be times of great stress, possibly not uniformly evil, or continuously evil, but times pockmarked with physical and mental and spiritual anguish for the Christian believer. The hardness of the times is not due to war or famine or plague, but the wicked ways and habits of unbelievers.

Persecution, however, is limited by God, not by the enemies, and not even by Satan himself. The story of Job begins with Satan seeking an audience with God, asking for permission to persecute this servant of God—"Then Satan answered the LORD and said, "Does Job fear God for no reason? Have you not put a hedge around him and his house and all that he has, on every side? You have blessed the work of his hands, and his possessions have increased in the land. But stretch out your hand and touch all that he has, and he will curse you to your face." And the LORD said to Satan, "Behold, all that he has is in your hand. Only against him do not stretch out your hand." So Satan went out from the presence of the LORD." (Job 1:9–12) Notice the limited amount of time in Revelation 2:10—"ten days." Jesus tells us in Matthew 10:28: "Do not be afraid of those who kill the body but cannot kill the soul. Rather be afraid of the One who can destroy both soul and body in hell."

Finally, persecution for the sake of righteousness is a *privilege*! "You can be glad when that happens—give a cheer, even!—for though they don't like it, I do! And all heaven applauds. And know that you are in good company. My prophets and witnesses have always gotten into this kind of trouble." Success in serving Christ can first be determined by *collision with the world*. James Denney puts it this way: "It is the work of God's Word to produce a new character, not only distinct from that of the unconverted but antagonistic to it, so that to the extent that we experience the power of God's Word, we come into collision with the world that rejects it."[6] The first question to ask in evaluating true discipleship is, therefore, what do your gospel enemies say? (1 Thes. 2:1–6; vv. 14–16)

Persecution for Christ is to be *expected,* Paul wrote to the Thessalonian Church in 1 Thessalonians 2:1, 2, 14–16 — "Remember the word that I said to you: 'A servant is not greater than his master.' If they persecuted me, they will also persecute you. If they kept my word, they will also keep yours." "I have said these things to you, that in me you may have peace. In the world you will have tribulation. But take heart; I have overcome the world." "Strengthening the souls of the disciples, encouraging them to continue in the faith, and saying that through many tribulations we must enter the kingdom of God." (John 15:20; 16:33; Acts 14:22)

How should you and I respond to persecution, even to intense persecution? There are "persecution pitfalls" to avoid. The first pitfall is the notion that "toleration will win the day." That is a false notion based on a false premise with a lie at its root. Toleration in their day and toleration in our day was only for those who were *not* evangelical, Bible based, Christ-centered people. Satan loves the secular premise of toleration and uses it for the destruction of God's people.

The second pitfall to watch out for is the thinking that "compromise is an option." This was the Pergamum problem referred to in Revelation 2:14-16. The Balaamites and Nicolaitans were advocating peaceful coexistence with the secular pagan society of their day. While we do not know precisely what these heresies were, we know that they were geared to deceiving Christian people to compromise their faith standards, just as Balaam advised the Midianite women in Israel's day to seduce and tempt them away from God (Numbers 25 and 31). Christ will have none of it. He commands them to repent!

The third pitfall is the fear of physical death, that we must avoid physical persecution and death at all costs. It's a pitfall because physical death is not the end. It is the "second death" (Rev. 2:11) that is the final end, and all faithful Christians will not experience that eternal separation from God.

What truths can we live by in facing persecution? Jesus has already overcome all persecution! This is the powerful message of the One who calls Himself, the "first and the last" the One who "died and came to life again" (Rev. 2:8). The One who has the sharp, double edged sword of final judgment and punishment of all of our oppressors (Rev. 2:12). Yes, there is the earthly ruler sword that Christ-followers may have to endure, but Christ has the ultimate sword, ultimate power, ultimate sovereignty.

Second, human suffering, even death, is not the end. The "crown of life" is given to those who so suffer. (Rev. 2:10) It's not over until it's really over! Third, God's "secrets" are with those who persevere. He talks about "hidden manna" and a "white stone with a new name on it." in Rev. 2:17. While many commentators speculate as to what these could be, what is true is that God will especially equip and speak to and bless those who overcome. If you read *Martyr's Mirror* you will find story after story of people across the world, in every age of the church, who in the midst of bodies being burned, or pulled apart, or loved ones killed in their presence, God's special peace and support were there for them.

So, if you are being persecuted for your faith in Christ, be encouraged!

Fear not! Look to the Risen Christ for overcoming faith and power!

Self Reflection & Discussion
1. How well do you endure persecution? Cite examples.
2. In what ways are modern Christians in American persecuted for their faith?
3. Have you been persecuted for your stand for Christ and his Word? How so?
4. How can we help our brothers and sisters around the world being persecuted for their faith in Christ?

Additional Note on Resisting Temptation Successfully (Matthew 4:1–11; James 1:13–18)
It is extremely easy in times of persecution to recant and side with those who want to destroy our faith in Christ. Temptation is a powerful enemy. How do we successfully conquer temptation in our lives?

We must acknowledge the reality of the inward battle — "In our members there is a slumbering inclination toward desire which is both sudden and fierce. With irresistible power desire seizes mastery over the flesh. All at once a secret, smoldering fire is kindled. The flesh burns and is in flames. It makes no difference whether it is sexual desire or ambition or vanity or desire for revenge or love of fame and power or greed for money . . . At this moment God is quite unreal to us. He loses all reality, and only desire for the creature is real. . . The powers of clear discrimination and of decision are taken from us." (Dietrich Bonhoffer)

Temptation affects all of us and is always present in life (James 1:13; Matthew 4:1). Temptation has no age discrimination. The older and more mature in Christ we get, the more subtle and devious are the temptations.

Temptation is never caused by God, either directly or indirectly (James 1:13f). The Greek term is a neutral term dependent on the subject. So, when referring to God, it means testing. When referring to Satan, it means tempting, an enticement to do wrong, to destroy God's work in our lives. See Job. Temptation follows a consistent pattern (James 1:14-15; Matthew 4:2) which consists of (1) the bait; (2) the desire; and,

(3) the allurement.

We overcome temptation first by knowing Jesus Christ as our victory over temptation (Hebrews 2:17, 18). We overcome temptation by living God's truth (cf. Matthew 4:4; 1 Corinthians 10:13; Ephesians 6:11). This is not just generalizing truth, but making God's truth concrete and direct to our situation. Thus, if the temptation is despair, we are to put on the armor of faith. If it is spiritual error, the armor of knowledge (of the Word of God). If it is anger, the armor of gentleness and self-control.

We overcome temptation by knowing the Devil's tricks like rationalizing or misquoting the Bible itself! (cf. Matthew 4:7). We overcome temptation by actively resisting Satan's temptations (James 4:7; 1 Peter 5:8,9). Such resistance is both verbal and conscious.

The key is to "ride out the storm of temptation upon the encouragements of the Gospel."

Addendum: Modern Spiritual Warfare[7]

Most Christians know that we are engaged in a daily spiritual battle with Satan. Not only do we experience the onslaught of satanic attacks, deception and trickery, but we are told in the Scriptures that we must expect such challenges to our faith (cf. Eph. 6:10–18; 1 Thes. 2:18; James 4:7; 1 Pet. 5:8, 9). The constant, unrelenting fight against the evil triumvirate—the world, flesh and Devil—has indeed been well recorded in the history and lives of believers. Historically, such battle has been accomplished by prayer, Scripture, obedience, and reliance on God as well as other Christians.

Today, however, "spiritual warfare" has become a shorthand for various power encounters with "demons of despair," bitterness, lust, or any other sin you can name. This battle uses "spiritual mapping," a process of discerning the location of focused spiritual evil in a place or physical location. Marital problems, division among people, illnesses and many other problems and difficulties are treated as "satanic attacks" to be repulsed by confronting evil in intense prayer. Deliverance can be obtained by confessing and forsaking not only known sins, but also "ancestral sins." These sins have their root in ancestral curses that have been passed down from parents to children, from generation to generation. In some cases, such deliverances have been accompanied by faintings, prostrations, compulsive animal sounds and other phenomena. While a few churches have experienced what seems like genuine renewal through such warfare, others question the theology, psychology and results. What makes up authentic spiritual warfare? What about "ancestral sins?" Should I be expecting "weird" physical or emotional effects in the lives of people?

Use critical but nonjudgmental discernment

We must always "test the spirits to see whether they are from God," knowing that we have "an anointing from the Holy One" that allows us to "know the truth" (1 Jn. 4:1; 2:20f). In the explosive period of revival in New England from 1739 to 1742, Jonathan Edwards, arguably the greatest American theologian of revival, noted that a person or church doctrinally correct, but without a "sense of the gloriousness of God in his heart" must not go on unchallenged.[8]

Emotional response, however, is no firm proof of the Spirit's work. Strange bodily effects prove nothing. Edwards again noted they are neither sure signs of the Spirit's work nor delusions from the Devil. They are "simply indifferent—a kind of accidental package surrounding the real core of spiritual awakening."[9] Edwards says what really matters is that the heart is touched by the Spirit, issuing forth in a more certain faith, a deeper sensitivity to sin, an illumined mind, and a humble love for others.[10] The Devil will always seek to counterfeit a true movement of the Holy Spirit, usually through "excesses and extravagances."[11] Richard Lovelace points out that "it is in the Devil's interest to make Christians weird. ... The goal of his strategy is to create a church that is so institutionally strange that unbelievers will detour around it."[12]

On the other hand, critical assessment does not mean judgmentalism. God cannot be confined by our human understanding of orthodoxy. God is a God of wonderful surprises, often producing amazing effects on the whole person. Don't be hasty to judge what you have never experienced. Yes, we need to see if deliverances claimed result in lasting spiritual fruit. But this will take time and plenty of patience.

Focus on Christ and the Scriptures

In the matter of guidance and comfort for a band of discouraged and somewhat disillusioned disciples, Jesus prayed for them to be "sanctified by the truth" adding, "your word is truth"(Jn. 17:17). Spirit-driven warfare must be conducted by the Spirit of truth, who always works in and through the Scriptures. This was Jesus' legacy to the Church for all time. In wrestling with satanic temptation, Jesus stops the Devil with the written Word of the living God (cf. Matt. 4).

Casting out demons by the declaration of Jesus' Name is not a magical incantation nor a religious "impression" but rather the powerful Word of the living God coming to bear on satanic manifestation, delusion and trickery. Clinton Arnold, professor of New Testament at Talbot School of Theology, believes "spiritual warfare is biblical in relation to casting out demons. Yet, he says, spiritual mapping is 'nowhere modeled explicitly or implicitly in the Old or New Testament nor throughout church history."[13] Moreover, the biblical theology of warfare, inclusive of spiritual warfare, emphasizes King Jesus as the present reigning and coming Lord defeating the principalities and powers of this age (Col. 2:14, 15; 1 Cor.15:25, 26; 2 Thes. 2:3–12; cf. also Ps. 110:1).

David Powlison's main point in his book, *Power Encounters: Reclaiming Spiritual Warfare*, is that "demonization is never treated as moral evil."[14] "To treat patterns of sin by casting out demons subtly changes the terms of the universe toward one in which Satan's power is comparable to God's, and to one in which the responsibility of the sinner before God is confused."[15] Sin, at its heart, is humanistic rebellion against God's rule in our lives and our universe. It raises its ugly head at defiance of what God says in His Word. And it is that Word preached and taught and discipled through the mediating, powerful presence of the Holy Spirit that gives release with responsibility. Finally, the New Testament mandate to those who would preach and teach the Word of God is that they focus on "Christ and Him crucified" (1Cor. 2:1–5). Deliverance can be found only in the power of the resurrected Christ becoming Lord of my life, as He is of the universe in which I dwell.

Exercise exegetical care in biblical interpretation

Finally, a word to the pastor as student as well as teacher of God's Word. The case for the inheritance of demonic work in a person's life built upon a "troubling curse" in a parent or grandparent or beyond[16] is fraught with exegetical, hermeneutical and theological difficulties. While it is true that God created humanity as a "corporate race," with future generations affected with past behavior, it is not the case that the "sin of the fathers" passes directly to the children and beyond.

In Exodus 20:5 (cf. Deut. 5:9) the consequences of sin affect offspring only as they show contempt and rebellion as their fathers— "of those who hate me." A careful reading of the covenant stipulations in the Old Testament reveals that each generation had to obey God's terms for the blessings to apply to them. Heathen Nineveh, for one generation, was spared God's just judgment under Jonah's preaching because that particular generation repented. Succeeding generations failed to repent and thus reaped God's wrath (cf. Jonah vs. Nahum). Yes, the Old Testament exile took place because of the accumulation of sins of one generation after another. And, breaches of God's law by one generation do indeed affect future generations to come. The natural consequences of pollution, immorality, slavery, and so forth are an expression of God's law in operation.

It is, however, an unwarranted stretch to say as Gary Jacabella of Spiritual Warfare Ministries does that "ancestral sin provides Satan with the cursed ground he needs to build a work of demonization. Just as sure as a troubling curse can be inherited, so a demonic work built on such a curse of punishment can also be inherited."[17] Generational disobedience meant judgment for that generation. This is why it was so crucial for parents to teach God's covenantal requirements to each succeeding generation (cf. Deut. 4:9; 6:1ff). This is also why Ezekiel 3:4 reads in the Hebrew — "You see, every person stands in relation to me. The parent as a personal entity and the child as a personal entity relate to me in the same direct way. It is the person who sins that will die."[18] This does not deny Israel's corporate identity, nor excuse the sins of previous generations, but past generational sins could not be fatalistically blamed for present judgment, according to Ezekiel 3.

The curse of God was not "automatic" nor irrespective of present obedience or disobedience. Moreover, Jeremiah (Jer.31:29–30) predicted an eschatological day (our day) in which a visitation of the sins of the parents upon their offspring would have no place. In the New Testament passage, Rom. 5:12ff, we are not held guilty for the "one sin of the one man Adam" because of our corporate solidarity with him. It is a matter of the (immediate) imputation of Adam's sin to us that makes us guilty. We are "constituted sinners" (v.19) due to the representative relationship in which Adam stands.[19] In similar manner, Jesus' righteousness blesses all who trust him not because of the "same corporate link that God created and sees,"[20] but rather it is a legally imputed righteousness reckoned to the believer's account out of the free grace of God (cf. Rom. 5:15ff with 3:24–26 and the classic meaning of justification).

Claiming exegetical and theological justification for deliverances from Satan's power when the sins of parents and ancestors are confessed and renounced in Jesus' Name cannot be sustained. This does not necessarily deny what experientially happens. However, finding warrant from a supposed grid of covenantal theology or a defective view of how we inherit original sin cannot be verified in the literature and studies of historical, biblical theology.

The Alaskan bull moose males battle for dominance during the fall mating season. The strongest, heftiest moose, with the largest and strongest antlers, triumphs. The one that consumes the best diet in the summer, therefore, is the one who wins. As Craig Larson says, "Spiritual battles await all of us. Satan will choose a season to attack. Will we be victorious, or will we fall? Much depends on what we do now — before the wars begin. The bull-moose principle: Enduring faith, strength, and wisdom for trials are best developed before they're needed."[21]

Notes

1.   Some commentators separate verse 10 from verses 11–12, making the latter verses a "ninth" beatitude, noting that although verses 11–12 are an elaboration of verse 10, "its original independence from the preceding collection of eight is indicated not only by its different form but also by the use of the second person pronoun rather

than the third. Matthew probably received it in the form in which it stands and added it to the collection he had received from another source." (Donald Hagner, *Matthew 1–13, Word Biblical Commentary*, Vol. 33A (Zondervan, 2015), 95–96.) I treat them in the usual way as one beatitude on persecution.

2. Some of this material can be seen also in the author's "Facing Your Enemies: The Message from Smyrna & Pergamum," *Church Warnings! The Seven Churches of Revelation for Today* (Lulu Press, 2017), 45 – 56, as well as "Authentic Christian Service: Servant Leadership," *Authentic Christianity: The Message to the Thessalonians* (Lulu Press, 2019), 33–38.

3. Examples from the website of the Alliance Defense Fund, http://adflegal.org/.

4. Hagner, *Word Biblical Commentary*, 95.

5. Thomas Watson, "Concerning Persecution," *The Beatitudes: An Exposition of Matthew 5:1-12*, 1660, Monergism eBook, https://www.monergism.com/topics/free-ebooks.

6. Geoffrey B. Wilson, *New Testament Commentaries, Volume (Philippians to Hebrews and Revelation)*, quoting James Denney, Banner of Truth, 2005.

7. This section taken from the author's book, *Upfront and Indepth: Deeper Devotional Studies on Psalm 119* (Lulu Press, 2010).

8. From the sermon, "A Divine and Supernatural Light," preached by Jonathan Edwards, 1734, as noted by Richard Lovelace, "The Surprising Works of God: Jonathan Edwards on Revival, Then and Now" (*Christianity Today*, 1995).

9. From *Distinguishing Marks of A Work of the Spirit of God* (1741) as noted by Lovelace in the above article.

10. Lovelace.

11. See J. Edwards, *Treatise on the Religious Affections* (1744), as quoted by R. Lovelace.

12. Lovelace.

13. Andres Tapia, "Is the World Ripe for Revival?" in *Christianity Today*, 1994.

14. Tim Stafford, in a review of *Power Encounters: Reclaiming Spiritual Warfare*, by David A. Powlison (*Christianity Today*, 1995).

15. *Ibid.*

16. From Gary Jacabella, *Ancestral Sin*, reprint from Spiritual Warfare Ministries, No. 5, P.O. Box 396, Warrington, PA 18976.

17. *Ibid.*

18. Translation from Leslie C. Allen, *Ezekiel 1–19, Word Biblical Commentary*, WORD Pub., 1994. See his footnote 4a. for Hebrew explanation.

19. This explanation is from the classic systematic theologian, John Murray, in his rather technical, but extensive, *The Imputation of Adam's Sin*, Westminster Theological Seminary, Phila., PA.

20. Jacabella.

21. Craig B. Larson, "Spiritual Warfare" Illustration, *Leadership*, Vol. 9, No. 3.

Appendix

**Intimacy With God:
Knowing and Experiencing
God's Lavish Love**

Intimacy With God
Knowing And Experiencing God's Lavish Love

"See what kind of love the Father has given to us, that we should be called children of God; and so we are. The reason why the world does not know us is that it did not know him. Beloved, we are God's children now, and what we will be has not yet appeared; but we know that when he appears we shall be like him, because we shall see him as he is. And everyone who thus hopes in him purifies himself as he is pure."
(1 John 3:1–3, ESV)

Michael Slaughter, in his book, *Real Followers*, compares marriage like that of walking with Jesus.[1] He writes — "Carolyn and I struggled with our marriage for years. We seriously contemplated whether we should divorce. On June 1, 1992, our marriage totally turned around. On that date we both made a decision for unconditional commitment, no turning back, for better or worse, until death do us part. Although our marriage ceremony was almost twenty years earlier, my unconditional commitment did not occur until June 1, 1992."[2]

In like manner, a lot of people believe in Jesus. We call it a commitment because we believe an intellectual truth or because we have had an emotional experience. However, commitment is more than a mental judgment or an emotional experience. Sometimes people believe that because they "felt" something during worship, then God must have been there. Yet feelings change and commitments waver.

Slaughter and many others through the history of the Church are calling you and me to a radical, life-changing intimacy with God through Jesus Christ. The beatitudes of Jesus in Matthew 5 outline such a life. This kind of "beatitude-life" is so radical and so life changing that we gladly yield all we are and all we have to Christ and his cause in the world.

God created us for intimacy — "So God created man in his own image, in the image of God he created him; male and female he created them." (Genesis 1:27) God Himself would walk with the humans He created "in the cool of the day," just to fellowship and be close to them. Yet, when sin and rebellion entered through their choice to disobey God, humanity began a steady and sure track of separation from God. By Genesis 6 the old world had become so rebellious, so filled with violence and sin, so corrupt that the Bible says in Genesis 6:6 — "And the LORD regretted that he had made man on the earth, and it grieved him to his heart."

Sin became so heinous that the Hebrew text says it grieved God "into his heart." He felt "bitterly indignant," expressing the most intense form of human emotion, a mixture of rage and bitter anguish. The feeling would be similar to Dinah's brothers learning that their sister had been raped (Gen. 34:13), or to Jonathan's grief when he learned that Saul planned to kill David. This term is used only two other times expressive of God's feelings — "How often they rebelled against him in the wilderness and grieved him in the desert!" (Psalm 78:40) "But they rebelled and grieved his Holy Spirit; therefore he turned to be their enemy, and himself fought against them." (Isaiah 63:10) Ephesians 4:30 tells believers not to "grieve the Holy Spirit of God with whom you were sealed for the day of redemption." Yes, they may be what we call anthropomorphic terms, but there is no doubt that our Personal God "feels!"

Intimacy with God through the ages of biblical and Christian history has been always there for us. Think of the example and model of Enoch — "Enoch walked with God after he fathered Methuselah 300 years and had other sons and daughters. Thus all the days of Enoch were 365 years. Enoch walked with God, and he was not, for God took him." (Gen. 5:22–24) Think of the important saint and theologian, Augustine — "You have made us for yourself, O God, and our hearts are restless until they find their rest in You."[3] The old hymn *Be Thou My Vision*, puts it this way — "We taste Thee, O Thou Living Bread, And long to feast upon Thee still: We drink of Thee, the Fountainhead, And thirst our souls from Thee to fill."[4]

David Brainerd, the first American missionary to the Indians in the outlying territories beyond the settlements in Massachusetts, would describe it this way — "I retired pretty early for secret devotions; and in prayer, God was pleased to pour such ineffable comforts into my soul, that I could do nothing for some time but say over and over, O my sweet Savior! 'O my sweet Savior!' whom have I in heaven but thee? And there is none upon earth I desire besides thee.' . . . My soul never enjoyed so much of heaven before . . . I never felt so great a degree of resignation in my life."[5]

Samuel Rutherford, a seventeenth century Puritan in Scotland, wrote — "Oh, if my soul might but lie within the smell of His love; suppose I could get no more than the smell of it! O what a sight to be up in heaven, in that fair orchard of the new paradise, and to see and touch and kiss that ever-green Tree of Life! Woe, woe is me! That sin has made so many madmen, seeking the fool's paradise . . . Christ, Christ, nothing but Christ can cool our love's burning languor. O thirst love! Drink and spare not and be drunken with Christ!"[6]

A.W. Tozer in *The Pursuit of God* notes that —

[in our day] Christ may be 'received' without any special love for Him in the soul of the receiver. The man is 'saved,' but he is not hungry nor thirsty after God . . . The modern scientist has lost God amid the wonders of His world; we Christians are in real danger of losing God amid the wonders of His Word. God is a person, and, as such, can be cultivated as any person can. . . . in the midst of this great chill there are some . . . who will not be content with shallow logic. They will admit the force of the argument, and then turn away with tears to hunt some lonely place and pray, 'O God, show me thy glory.' They want to taste, to touch with their hearts, to see with their inner eyes the wonder that is God.[7]

Thomas DeWitt Talmage has said, "God puts his ear so close to you that He can hear your faintest whisper."[8]

How can we reclaim intimacy with God? How can we restore what was lost through intellectual contracts and vapid emotionalism? God Himself has made a way. He desires intimacy with us so much that the

Apostle John writes, "Consider how lavish is the love which the Father has showered upon us, that we should be called God's children! And that is what we are." (1 John 3:1) God himself restores intimacy by his selfless, sacrificial giving of his one and only Son for us, on our behalf. The writer John speaks with astonishment and emotional fervor and power and tells us about this great, reclaiming love of God for rebellious and sinful people like you and me.

Note that such love is *real and visible*. "Consider," or "look and see" how demonstrable God's love really is — "Beloved, let us love one another, for love is from God, and whoever loves has been born of God and knows God. Anyone who does not love does not know God, because God is love. In this the love of God was made manifest among us, that God sent his only Son into the world, so that we might live through him." (1 John 4:7–9) Such love is "out of this world;" it is lavish. We use that word to indicate something awesome, special and even supernatural. "Lavish" means "out of country." Such love is "showered upon us," poured out on us. It is a love we can see, experience and know, intimately know — "And that is what we are!"

The problem we have with intimacy is not a problem with God. He is right here, right now, giving all kinds of signals, inward and outward, for us to become intimate with him. Just like a marriage gone stale and dry and withered up, so our relationship with God becomes that way. God tells us in his Word that any choice less than intimacy with him, less than full and first commitment to him, is nothing less than spiritual adultery. Faithless Israel is called "idolaters" in Jeremiah — "Return, faithless people, declares the Lord, for I am your husband." (Jeremiah 3:14)

Idolatry doesn't just mean placing something in creation above God in our minds. It also means separating ourselves from his heart, tearing ourselves from his embrace, choosing another husband, another lover, another way to fulfill our desires. Intimacy barriers are really idols after which we lust like adulterers! There are four intimacy barriers to consider.

The first intimacy barrier is duty for duty's sake. John Piper has well said, "For many, Christianiy has become the grinding out of general doctrinal laws from collections of biblical facts. But childlike wonder and awe have died. The scenery and poetry and music of the majesty of God have dried up like a forgotten peach at the back of a refrigerator."[9] Michael Slaughter points out that many Christians are "studying concepts. Churches and Christians have become concept-centered. We study what God said to Moses, what God said to David, what Jesus said to his disciples, what Paul said to the churches of his day. Because we have become concept-centered by studying principles, we are not Christ-centered and Holy Spirit-centered. We're missing what God is saying to us today."[10] For instance, have classes on parenting made you a better, more godly, more Christ-like parent? Have classes on holiness made you more holy? Have classes on the millennium made you thrill at the prospect of Jesus coming again and made you, therefore, ready for his return?

A second intimacy barrier is depending on a past act for a present reality. God calls us to a "now" relationship with himself — "When the Spirit of truth comes, he will guide you into all the truth, for he will not speak on his own authority, but whatever he hears he will speak, and he will declare to you the things that are to come." (John 16:13) Have you been hearing about the things that are to come from God the Holy Spirit? Or, has your doctrinal laden past prevented you from anticipating the future?

A third intimacy barrier is the "see-saw" of emotionalism. We let our good or bad emotions dictate our view of God and his love. God loves us when things are going well for us, and God does not love us when things are going badly for us. Jesus, on the other hand, said in John 15 — "If you abide in me, and my words abide in you, ask whatever you wish, and it will be done for you. . . . These things I have spoken to you, that my joy may be in you, and that your joy may be full." (John 15:7, 11) Genuine intimacy gives stability and assurance of God's presence, no matter what our situation or emotions.

A final intimacy barrier is harboring grudges or possessing a complaining spirit. We so easily forget the prescription of Psalm 37 — "Fret not yourself because of evildoers; be not envious of wrongdoers! For they will soon fade like the grass and wither like the green herb. Trust in the LORD, and do good; dwell in the land and befriend faithfulness.

Delight yourself in the LORD, and he will give you the desires of your heart." (Psalm 37:1–4)

I end with two prayers for intimacy from servants of God who discovered the highly intimate God. Pray them with me this day —

O God, I have tasted thy goodness
and it has both satisfied me and made me thirsty for more.
I am painfully conscious of my need for further grace.
I am ashamed of my lack of desire.
O God, the Triune God, I want to want Thee;
I long to be filled with longing;
I thirst to be made more thirsty still.
Show me Thy glory, I pray Thee, that so I may
know Thee indeed. Begin in mercy a new work of love
within me. Say to my soul, "Rise up, my love,
my fair one, and come away." Then give me grace to rise
and follow Thee from this misty lowland
where I have wandered so long.
In Jesus' Name, Amen.[11]

Lord, I want to be a real follower of Jesus
under your command.
I will no longer be my own.
I will give myself up to you in all areas.
Lord, make me all that you can.
I put myself fully into your hands.
Put me to doing; put me to suffering.
Let me be employed for you, or laid aside for you.
Let me be full; let me be empty.
Let me have all things; let me have nothing.
I freely and with a willing heart
give all to your pleasure and disposal.
Amen.[12]

Notes

1. Michael Slaughter, *Real Followers: Beyond Virtual Christianity* (Nashville: Abingdon Press, 1999).

2. *Ibid.*

3. "Still he desires to praise thee, this man who is only a small part of thy creation. Thou hast prompted him, that he should delight to praise thee, for thou hast made us for thyself and restless is our heart until it comes to rest in thee." (Augustine, *Confessions*, Book 1, Part 1)

4. "Be Thou My Vision" (Old Irish: *Rop tú mo baile* or *Rob tú mo bhoile*) is a traditional Christian hymn of Irish origin. The words are based on a Middle Irish poem often attributed to the sixth-century Irish Christian poet Dallán Forgaill, although it is probably later than that. The best-known English version, with some minor variations, was translated by Eleanor Hull and published in 1912." (https://en.wikipedia.org/wiki/Be_Thou_My_Vision)

5. Jonathan Edwards, ed., *The Life and Diary of David Brainerd* (Massachusetts: Hendrikson Publishers, 2006).

6. A. A. Bonar, *The Letters of Samuel Rutherford* (Forgotten Books, 2012 reprint) and *Letters of Samuel Rutherford* (Banner of Truth, 2006 reprint of 1664 edition).

7. A. W. Tozer, "Following Hard After God, " Chapter 1, *The Pursuit of God* (Harrisburg, PA: Christian Publications, 1948, reprinted by Aneko Press, 2015).

8. Cheri Fuller, "Promised Help," Feb. 14 Devotional, by Thomas Talmage (1832–1902), *The One Year Book of Praying Through the Bible* (Tyndale House Publishers, 2003). "God puts his ear so closely down to your lips that He can hear your faintest whisper. It is not God away off up yonder. It is God away down here, close up, so close up that when you pray to him, it is more a whisper than a kiss."

9. John Piper, *Desiring God: Meditations of A Christian Hedonist* (Colorado Springs: Multnomah Press, 1986, 1996, 2003, 2011), 100.

10. Slaughter, 44, 45.

11. Tozer, *The Pursuit of God*.

12. Slaughter, *Real Followers*.

Other Titles
By The Author

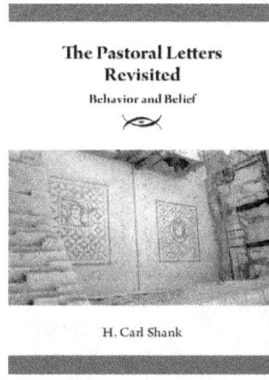

The Pastoral Letters Revisited: Behavior and Belief, 2018.

The three New Testament letters, 1 Timothy, 2 Timothy and Titus, are what we call the Pastoral Epistles. Timothy and Titus were young, energetic, trustworthy and effective as Christian workers and leaders. They were both called to difficult and challenging situations. Timothy was more shy than Titus, but both needed encouragement and instruction as how to handle false teachers and difficult questions of pastoral conduct and leadership.

This book is not an exhaustive commentary or study on the Pastoral Epistles. It is rather a close look at some of the major themes of these letters.

Available from lulu.com and amazon.com and other booksellers.

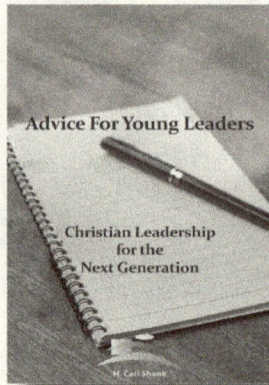

Advice for Young Leaders: Christian Leadership for the Next Generation, 2018.

Francis Schaeffer once said and wrote that we live and minister before a "watching world." The non-Christian world often wants us to stumble and falter and fail. They want committed believers in Jesus Christ to betray their Lord and Savior. They watch for it, wait for it and then report it when it happens as evidence of moral and institutional failure and sickness. The real question for those daring to enter into full-time professional ministerial service for the Lord Jesus Christ is how do I not fall and finally fail my Lord and Savior? How do I make sure that my ministry years will be biblically fruitful and that I will remain faithful to Christ? How can I leave a legacy of godliness and faithfulness that others can follow safely and surely? This book explores some of the answers to those questions.

Available from lulu.com and amazon.com and other booksellers.

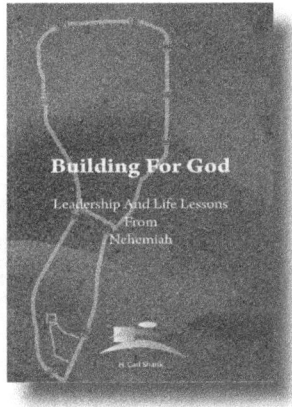

Building For God: Leadership and Life Lessons from Nehemiah, A Bible Study, 2018.

Nehemiah was an unknown servant to a great ancient Near Eastern king, a cupbearer by trade. He was not a famous Jewish prophet, scribe or known leader. Yet, through this man, the torn down and burnt walls of Jerusalem were rebuilt in an amazing fifty-two days. He faced opposition and ridicule by the appointed leaders on the ground in and around Jerusalem. He had to deal with recalcitrant people, scared people and lazy, unproductive people. He had to conquer unfair business practices and engineer conflict resolution, all while facing enemies from a secular empire.

Available from lulu.com and amazon.com and other booksellers.

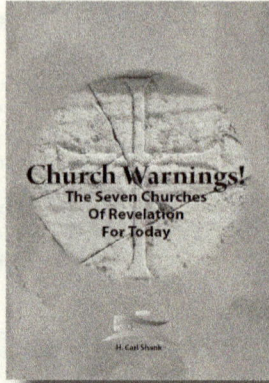

Church Warnings! The Seven Churches of Revelation for Today, A Bible Study, 2017.

A Bible study with Teacher Notes and discussion guide on the seven churches cited in Revelation 2–3. Christ's messages to the seven churches of Revelation are as relevant today as they were then. Ephesus-like churches who have "forsaken their first love," and churches like Pergamum and Thyatira which tolerate false teachers and teaching, as well as churches like Sardis and Laodicea who are lackadaisical about the faith are in danger. Churches like Smyrna and Philadelphia who have endured much persecution are told to hold on and overcome. To all seven, Jesus says, "He who has an ear, let him hear what the Spirit says to the churches."

Available from lulu.com and amazon.com and other booksellers.

Jonah: A Reluctant Messenger, A Needy People, and God's Amazing Grace, A Bible Study, 2017.

A Bible study and discussion guide on the Old Testament story of Jonah. Grace transforms everything it touches. It does not discriminate, based on race, tradition, church experience, selectability, preference, timing or worth. There is no sin so great that grace cannot conquer and transform. There is no life so lost that grace cannot find and reclaim it. There is no one so wicked or unworthy that grace cannot totally change and renovate. This study of Jonah shows God's amazing, mighty and magnificent grace.

Available from lulu.com and amazon.com and other booksellers.

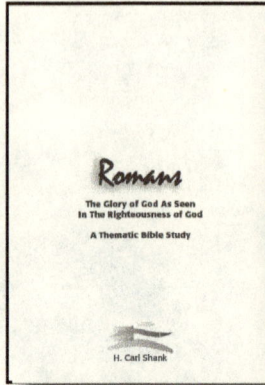

Romans: The Glory of God As Seen in the Righteousness of God, A Thematic Bible Study, 2017.

A Bible study book on Romans with Leader's Notes. The study is arranged according to the themes of Paul's Letter to the Romans. "Righteousness From A Sovereign God," "Universal Guilt," "Gospel Benefits," "Sanctification: God's Picture of Righteousness In Our Lives," "Sovereignty: God's Sovereignty Leads to Grateful Praise and Gospel Love," "Understanding God's Sovereign Purposes," "God Is Not Through With Israel," "Living Sacrifices," "The Politically Correct Christian," and "Liberty Not License."

Available from lulu.com and amazon.com and other booksellers.

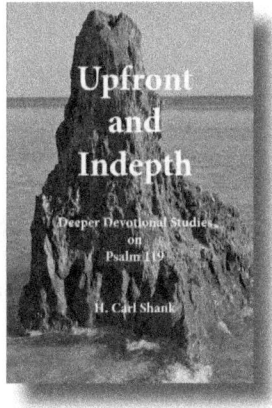

Upfront and Indepth: Deeper Devotional Studies on Psalm 119, 2010.

This little exposition of Psalm 119 unlocks some of the deeper truths of the longest Psalm recorded in the Bible. Not for the tame, or for a quick read, this devotional study will challenge you to personally go places you have never visited within your own walk with God.

Available from lulu.com and amazon.com and other booksellers.

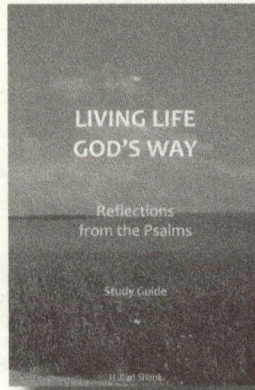

Living Life God's Way: Reflections from the Psalms, 2016.

This is a study guide for selected Psalms from the Bible. It's fill-in-the blanks format is perfect for a small group study, or even a personal study of the Psalms. It references 67 of the most read Psalms and includes a special study of Psalm 1. A selection of "Psalms for Christmas" is included in the study.

Available from lulu.com and amazon.com and other booksellers. A *Leader's Guide* is also available.

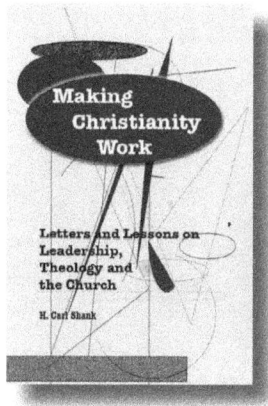

Making Christianity Work: Letters and Lessons on Leadership, Theology and the Church, 2012.

Insights shared by the author from letters, emails and various mentoring situations involving a number of lay and professional ministry leaders over an almost forty year span. Sections include "Feelings About God and Life," "Knowing God Better," "Faith and Culture," "On Church Health and Growth," "On Church Difficulties," "On Preaching and Teaching," and "On Theology."

Available from lulu.com and amazon.com and other booksellers.

www.ingramcontent.com/pod-product-compliance
Lightning Source LLC
Chambersburg PA
CBHW031326040426
42443CB00005B/236